ADDRESSING HOMELESSNESS AND HOUSING INSECURITY IN HIGHER EDUCATION

ADDRESSING HOMELESSNESS AND HOUSING INSECURITY IN HIGHER EDUCATION

STRATEGIES FOR EDUCATIONAL LEADERS

Ronald E. Hallett
Rashida M. Crutchfield
Jennifer J. Maguire

Foreword by Timothy P. White

Published by Teachers College Press, 1234 Amsterdam Avenue, New York, NY 10027

Cover design by adam b. bohannon. Cover photo by AlexRaths / iStock by GettyImages.

Library of Congress Cataloging-in-Publication Data is available at loc.gov

ISBN 978-0-8077-6143-4 (paper)
ISBN 978-0-8077-6183-0 (hardcover)
ISBN 978-0-8077-7780-0 (ebook)

Printed on acid-free paper
Manufactured in the United States of America

Contents

Foreword

About 4 years ago, I had the opportunity to meet Aaron Green. When I met Aaron, he was graduating from California State University, Long Beach. His years of study had not been easy. This young man, a former foster youth, had gone without food many times in his academic career. Stable housing was a constant challenge. He faced these and many other obstacles on his road to graduation. Yet, he overcame every challenge—with the help of the campus community—and now he is helping others in a career in his community.

Aaron's story highlights the hurdles our students continue to face, even after they begin their degree program. Many face health issues. Many must care for others. Many struggle to balance work and study. Many go for days—or much longer—without adequate food and shelter.

Housing insecurity, homelessness, and food insecurity affect students at conceivably every college and university throughout the United States. We know from research that California's institutions of higher education are no exception. Since 2015, the California State University has led efforts to further study the scope and impact of food and housing insecurity, share best practices with colleagues across our campuses and nationally, and continue to deploy real-world, innovative solutions that directly assist students today, tomorrow, and in the future.

As the chancellor of the California State University (CSU), the largest system of senior higher education in the country, with 23 campuses, 50,000 faculty and staff, and 484,000 students, I am acutely aware of my role in leadership to address this urgent issue. We as presidents, chancellors, and leaders across the nation have the opportunity to increase the emerging awareness of basic needs insecurity. We can shift the narrative of the "starving student" as a rite of passage in higher education and meet our responsibility to respond to the diversity of our student populations by ensuring that their efforts toward graduation are supported with care and concern for their well-being.

Indeed, I recall with gratitude that I received community assistance for both housing and food when I was an undergraduate student 5 decades ago. This assistance enabled me to stay on track and graduate in a timely fashion.

These are our students. These are the strivers who will define for a generation what it means to radically change the course of one's life. We must do all that we can to ensure that they have a place in this world where they can go when they are hungry and have no place to sleep.

The book you are about to read by Dr. Ronald E. Hallett, Dr. Rashida M. Crutchfield, and Dr. Jennifer J. Maguire is here to help you address the needs of your students and, ultimately, to support your missions for student success. It provides an excellent overview of housing insecurity and homelessness, which can ground your perspective on who our students are and the experiences they might be enduring. This book provides context, but it also offers tangible suggestions for how you can develop or expand your philosophical, practical, and political efforts to address the needs of students.

I met with Dr. Crutchfield during her work assessing these social problems in the California State University system and later Dr. Maguire as she joined in leadership in this study. Along with Dr. Hallett, their efforts in research and with this book are supporting the creation of conditions that allow our students to succeed. Years of research have shown the impact of basic needs insecurity on student well-being. Students facing instability endure untenable obstacles and negative repercussions on their physical and mental health as well as their academic outcomes. This book enables readers to more fully understand the realities their students face and the role they have in supporting them. It will help staff, faculty, administrators, and community partners address the needs of students, create or revise current policy and practice, and encourage the utilization of various strategies in order to retain students to graduation.

As the chancellor of the CSU system, I support the efforts of our students, staff, faculty, and administrators across our 23 campuses who are supporting almost a half a million students here in California. Increasingly, it is clear that strong and enduring partnerships with community agencies and organizations are essential. Indeed, success in addressing basic needs and student wellness can and does happen with your commitment and the collaborative initiatives you develop each and every day. The information, narratives, resources, and strategies offered in this book will prove to be an invaluable resource to our work as we reach our students. This book will be a welcome addition to your repertoire of sources.

—Chancellor Timothy P. White,
The California State University

CHAPTER 1

Introduction

Homelessness and housing insecurity exist on college campuses across the United States. This reality will not surprise many educators who work closely with students and have assisted students as they struggle to attend class while being uncertain where they will sleep at night. These individuals negotiate economic, political, and social issues while pursuing postsecondary degrees and credentials. This constrains their ability to attain a college degree that gives them the best odds for long-term housing stability and overall health and well-being. The amount of support provided by postsecondary institutions, states, and the federal government depends upon the priorities of the leadership and policymakers, which are subject to change. When less support is available, students from low-income and marginalized backgrounds struggle to balance educational costs with meeting their basic needs. Conversely, more significant support allows them to dedicate more time and energy toward education without worrying about food and housing.

Issues related to food and housing insecurity among college students have likely existed for decades. However, their struggles have largely been invisible to policymakers and educational leadership. The common assumption has been that students in college may struggle a bit financially, but that process builds character that prepares them for future life. In the past few years, the real financial struggles of students in college have become evident to colleges and universities. The current economic and political context makes the issue more obvious to researchers, administrators, and policymakers. The opportunity exists to leverage the current interest in basic needs insecurity to create policies and services that support students through the completion of a higher education degree.

This book provides information and tools for educators and higher education professionals to build effective institutional supports for college students facing housing insecurity. In this chapter, we introduce the idea that homelessness and housing insecurity are significant issues for postsecondary institutions across the United States. In addition, we explain how colleges and universities play an integral role in helping these students successfully achieve a degree that could lead to future residential stability. We explore aspects of access to college as well as issues related to persistence

The entire process of attending postsecondary education by basic needs insecurity. Throughout the book, we weave f students experiencing housing and food insecurity (such as below). Our hope is that their stories can serve as a reflection of how your students experience the challenges associated with homelessness and housing insecurity. We also provide insights from people who have been committed to serving these students in hopes that their experiences will support your work.

How Homelessness Influenced Miguel

Miguel, a first-year business major, planned to pursue a career in the entertainment industry. He arrived to campus several hours before class to take advantage of the free Internet and study space in the library. While highly capable, Miguel often struggled academically. In addition to navigating class expectations, he also had to figure out how to acquire food and housing each day. His father lived on the streets and his mother struggled with addiction, which undermined her residential stability. A few friends and family members allowed Miguel to stay with them for a night from time to time. When no place was available, he would sleep on a park bench on the edge of campus. The constant stress of mobility and hunger detracted from his academic pursuits. However, he believed that a college degree was his path to future stability. Miguel, like many college students, endured basic needs insecurity.

SIZE OF THE ISSUE

Postsecondary institutions have not been required by federal or state governments to capture the number of students experiencing housing insecurity. The only national-level statistics on prevalence available involve the number of individuals who mark "unaccompanied homeless" on the Free Application for Federal Student Aid (FAFSA). In the 2016–2017 application cycle, 32,739 individuals checked that box on the FAFSA application (National Center for Homeless Education [NCHE], 2017). While this number provides some useful information, most researchers and advocates argue that the narrow definitional parameters to qualify for this categorization significantly underestimate how many college students experience housing insecurity. To qualify as "unaccompanied homeless," the individual would need to be in high school at the time of the application and have someone, such as a homeless liaison for the school district, verify their status. In addition, the student would need to be living outside of a family unit and not be in the foster care system. If they are a current or prospective college student who is not in high school, they could also mark "homeless" on the FAFSA and go through a verification process with a financial aid administrator at their postsecondary institution. Many individuals who are experiencing homelessness and housing insecurity have a difficult time getting through the verification process with a district homeless liaison; the process becomes even more challenging when they attempt to qualify as a college student because they must get letters from professionals verifying their status and then go through an interview with a financial aid administrator (Crutchfield, Chambers, & Duffield, 2016). And others may not check the box because they avoid identifying as "homeless" due to social shame or lack of understanding that their housing situation may qualify as homeless (Hallett, 2012; Tierney, Gupton, & Hallett, 2008; Tierney & Hallett, 2012; Wolch et al., 2007). Beyond these stipulations, students experiencing housing insecurity who are already deemed "independent" on the FAFSA for a variety of reasons (e.g., veteran or marital status) are also not included in this number.

As we discuss in the next chapter, the process of identifying students experiencing housing insecurity is negatively impacted by stereotypical assumptions about what homelessness means. Students and practitioners may assume an individual is not homeless because they do not live in a shelter or a public space (e.g., car, street, or abandoned building). Understanding the complexity and diversity of housing insecurity will allow practitioners to make more accurate determinations about who qualifies for support. In addition, current and prospective students will need to be informed in order to know when they qualify for support.

Given the lack of federal data on homelessness and housing insecurity, several postsecondary institutions and research centers have conducted studies to understand the size and scope of basic needs insecurity among college students in the United States. Researchers generally take a more comprehensive approach to identifying individuals experiencing homelessness and housing insecurity, which results in significantly higher rates than noted on the FAFSA. As Table 1.1 illustrates, the emerging data suggest a significant proportion of students attending 2-year and 4-year institutions experience housing insecurity. These studies also suggest a correlation between housing and food insecurity. To clarify terminology, *housing insecurity* refers to any form of residential arrangement that is not adequate, stable, and safe, whereas *homelessness* involves a narrow focus on lack of housing that is similar to how the U.S. Department of Housing and Urban Development (HUD) defines the term. We unpack these concepts further in Chapter 2. The important takeaway at this point is that homelessness and housing insecurity appear to be significant issues that impact students across the nation who attend both 2-year and 4-year institutions.

Table 1.1. Size and Scope of Housing Insecurity in Higher Education

Context	Institution Type	Rate of Housing Insecurity	Homelessness	Citation
California sample of community colleges (90 campuses)	2-year	One-third of students experienced housing insecurity		Wood, Harris, & Delgado, 2017
National sample of community colleges (institutions from 24 states)	2-year	51–52% were housing insecure	13–14% experienced homelessness	Goldrick-Rab, Broton, & Eisenberg, 2015; Goldrick-Rab, Richardson, & Hernandez, 2017
Massachusetts higher education system	2-year and 4-year	45% of students experienced housing insecurity		Massachusetts Department of Higher Education, 2017
City University of New York (17 institutions)	2-year and 4-year	40% of students experienced housing insecurity		Tsui et al., 2011
California State University (all 23 campuses)	4-year		10.9% of students experienced homelessness	Crutchfield & Maguire, 2018
University of Massachusetts Boston	4-year	45% were housing insecure	5.4% experienced homelessness	Silva et al., 2017
University of California (10 campuses)			5% of undergraduate and graduate students experienced homelessness at some point during their enrollment	University of California Global Food Initiative, 2017

We encourage all institutions and statewide university systems to collect data on food and housing insecurity. Emerging data suggest that food and housing insecurity are significant issues that college students experience across the United States. However, the localized data are valuable as educational leaders and policymakers make decisions about how to support their students.

Campus Differences Within a University System

Institutional data often vary by campus. In the California State University (CSU) Study of Student Basic Needs (Crutchfiled & Maguire, 2018), the prevalence rate of homelessness varied significantly among campuses. Across the 23 CSU campuses, the average number of students who reported experiencing homelessness one or more times in the past 12 months ranged from 6.6% to 18.6%. Higher rates of homelessness were recorded at CSU campus locations known to have limited affordable housing options nearby.

IMPORTANCE OF HIGHER EDUCATION FOR FUTURE STABILITY

You may have heard people say something like, "Students experiencing homelessness should focus on stabilizing their life and then attend college once they are stable." We appreciate the sentiment behind this statement. The concern may be that students have complex challenges that negatively influence their postsecondary experience. The belief may be that regular class attendance and persistence until graduation will be impossible for these students until basic needs insecurity is resolved. The time, energy, and resources of the institution would be more effective if focused on students who already have achieved stability. Underlying this assumption is that higher education does not play a primary role in stabilizing basic needs insecurity and that a student cannot successfully complete coursework while also enduring housing insecurity. Others may argue that addressing basic needs insecurity is not the purpose or role of postsecondary institutions. Based upon our experiences and the voices of college students, we challenge these assumptions.

Most students experiencing housing insecurity consistently discuss how important postsecondary education is for their future stability (Tierney et al., 2008). They believe that earning a degree or credential increases the likelihood of securing gainful employment, avoiding sustained low-wage work, and achieving many other outcomes related to health and well-being (Ambrose, 2016; Dill & Lee, 2016; Gupton, 2017; Hallett & Freas, 2018; Hyatt, Walzer, & Julianelle, 2014; Schmitz, 2016). In most cities across the United States, individuals cannot secure stable housing by working a full-time minimum wage position. Students experiencing housing insecurity enter and persist in college in order to achieve their goals of personal growth, employment, and stable housing. Although they consistently identify completing a 4-year degree or higher as a goal, these students are 60% more likely than their stably housed peers to attend community college (Wood, Harris, & Delgado, 2017). Beyond economic stability, higher education offers students social and cultural experiences that enrich their lives and may provide hope for the future.

YOU PLAY AN IMPORTANT ROLE

While students experiencing housing insecurity may have potential, skill, and drive, they rely heavily on the support of instructors and educational professionals. The creation of supportive spaces allows students to find resources, refuge, and social engagement that enables them to share their stories of success and challenge. Often, the creation of these programs starts with committed champions and advocates who generate and maintain energy to build campus coalitions, seek sustainable support, and implement carefully crafted programmatic responses.

The overall environment on your campus influences if and how students ask for support. Building awareness and enthusiasm to create a campus climate that is accepting of students experiencing housing insecurity takes creativity and strategy. Your role is essential. Each campus context is different. Creating a team of dedicated and caring individuals who can explore issues on your campus is an important first step. As the issues your students experience become more clearly understood, you can find and expand ways to offer supports that will encourage their retention until graduation.

As an embedded institutional agent, you are in the best position to influence the culture. While we provide ideas throughout this book, your role in translating these ideas into practice at your institution is important. We encourage you to explore how to collaboratively craft and implement our recommendations into practice within your specific context.

PREVIEW OF THE BOOK

The purpose of this book is to translate the current body of research related to how homelessness and housing insecurity influences students' educational experiences into practical strategies that can be implemented on your campus. Continued work is needed to understand the issue of collegiate housing insecurity and how to best support retention for these students. Our goal is to highlight some promising practices while also identifying key areas that warrant continued attention. Drawing from decades of research and policy development, we begin by explaining and defining homelessness and housing insecurity within the higher education context. Chapter 2 includes a definitional continuum that can help practitioners and policymakers understand the complexity and size of the issue. Chapter 3 summarizes research related to how housing insecurity influences postsecondary education as well as policies that frame how these students experience higher education.

We introduce a trauma-informed model in Chapter 4 that allows practitioners and administrators to explore and address issues of homelessness and housing insecurity within the local context. The model includes four stages: localizing, evaluating, implementing, and sustaining. We then dedicate a chapter to each stage in order to carefully consider how an institution can use the model to support its students.

Application on Your Campus

Each chapter ends with a few prompts on how to apply the ideas within your campus context. Given the importance of carefully considering how local issues and resources frame student experiences, we do not provide prescriptive details. Rather, this portion of the book allows for you to explore ways to integrate the ideas on your campus.

As we will discuss later in the book, a collaborative approach tends to be the most successful. Involving individuals from across campus and also from the community allows for a more comprehensive assessment of the issue as well as a more thorough implementation of supports. We encourage you to consider gathering a team of individuals on campus to read this book together. The group could include a representative from admissions, student affairs, health/counseling, academic affairs, financial aid, registration, faculty, and student involvement. In particular, you may want to begin with individuals who already have an interest in the issue and can serve as advocates/champions of the cause as you move forward with presenting recommendations to the administration.

CHAPTER 2

Housing Insecurity in Higher Education

Supporting students experiencing homelessness and housing insecurity requires moving past common notions about what these terms mean. For most people, their primary encounters with homelessness occur when they see someone sleeping on the street or asking for money outside of a business. These individuals, who are often experiencing chronic homelessness, represent only a small portion of the homeless population and do not represent those who live in unstable or unsafe places. Most of the students attending your campus who experience homelessness and housing insecurity will not be living in these more public spaces. They may not even look the way you might expect someone to look who is homeless. Adopting a more nuanced and inclusive definition of housing insecurity will be an important first step to understanding the issue on your campus and determining what supports might be needed to encourage student retention until graduation.

Understanding basic needs insecurity requires moving away from beliefs that housing can be evaluated through binary assumptions that an individual is either housed or homeless. Student realities tend to be far more complex. We encourage you to consider housing a continuum that includes many different residential contexts. In the sections the follow, we discuss the Higher Education Housing Continuum before unpacking the four general housing formations that fit within the continuum.

HIGHER EDUCATION HOUSING CONTINUUM

Evaluating if a person is "homeless" or not can be difficult and problematic. Many unstable living conditions are not observable in the day-to-day interactions that students have with faculty, staff, and peers. Their experiences do not easily fit within a binary approach. There are students who have experienced intermittent or long-term homelessness prior to enrolling in higher education, while others may experience homelessness for the first time in college. Some individuals may have a place to stay, but the location can be inconsistent, unsafe, or inadequate. Students could have to move unexpectedly from their current residence due to eviction and not have the funds to afford another move. An unexpected life event may result in homelessness for students who have never experienced housing insecurity. Those students may be homeless for months, but find stable living circumstances over time. Taking an either/or approach does not capture the individuals who may have recently experienced residential instability and may still need support dealing with the traumas associated with housing insecurity. As we discuss later, these individuals may still need assistance as they adjust to stable housing.

Housing insecurity often involves transition between different living arrangements. We encourage you to consider a broader view of housing rather than a point-in-time assessment. A student who may appear stably housed in an apartment today may actually be moving between several different living arrangements every couple of weeks. Elizabeth's story illustrates the complexity and uncertainty associated with housing insecurity.

Elizabeth's First Time Being Homeless

Elizabeth, who was about to graduate with a degree in communicative sciences and deaf studies, grew up in a "middle income" family and had never experienced homelessness prior to college. When she started the semester, she had some financial aid, a job, and small contributions from her mother for college expenses. She budgeted for each semester and was stunned when her landlord evicted her and her roommates.

"And then come June, he tells us we need to be out of our house by the end of our lease, because he's selling the house. And so that put me in a hard position 'cause me paying for everything, I didn't set aside money for a deposit anywhere or anything. And so I ended up being homeless for about 4 months. Sleeping on friends' couches, staying in my car a couple nights. I kind of just bummed it on campus."

The Higher Education Housing Continuum (Hallett & Crutchfield, 2017) provides a more fluid and wholistic approach to considering college-student housing stability (see Figure 2.1). The continuum considers four different categories of housing: homelessness, housing instability, recent housing instability, and housing secure.

The arrows between the categories illustrate movement between different residential contexts. For some students, this may happen multiple times within an academic term. Note that the arrows move in both directions. While we hope students experiencing homelessness would steadily move toward housing security, that generally does not happen in a linear way. Students may find temporary housing for a short period and then lose it. In

Figure 2.1. Higher Education Housing Continuum

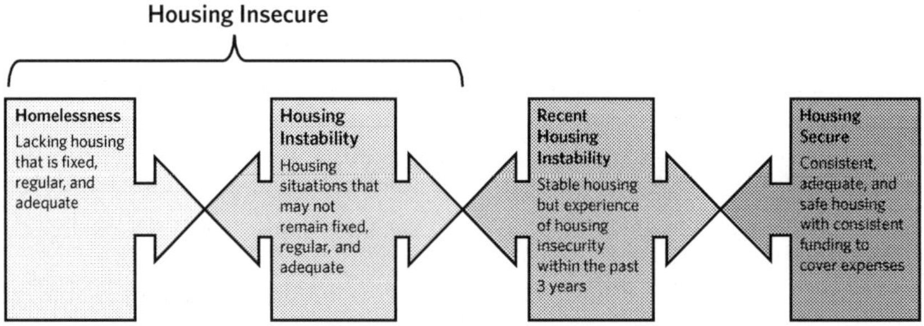

Housing Insecure

Homelessness
Lacking housing that is fixed, regular, and adequate

Housing Instability
Housing situations that may not remain fixed, regular, and adequate

Recent Housing Instability
Stable housing but experience of housing insecurity within the past 3 years

Housing Secure
Consistent, adequate, and safe housing with consistent funding to cover expenses

Note: Adapted from Hallett & Crutchfield (2017).

addition, some students will start college with secure and stable housing, but experience housing insecurity when something happens (e.g., loss of employment or family crisis).

In the sections that follow, we unpack each of these different housing experiences. Each category includes a definition, discussion, and illustrations. One university student shares what it is like to constantly be "on the move."

Chant'e Lived "on the Move"

I am a 39-year-old, first-generation, transfer student who earned a BA in sociology and an expected master's in social work in 2020. Twice homeless, as a teen and also as an incoming undergraduate, I found my passion as an activist for promoting housing as a human right.

Not having a home is so time-consuming and taxing on the body. My family would have to move our camp regularly because of restrictions at campsites. Our family utilized fee-based campsites because amenities often included showers, trash cans, and BBQ grills. If we were lucky, there might be an electrical outlet in a creepy bathroom where we could sit until our phones and computers charged. However, if we walked away, even for a moment, someone would likely steal our belongings. One of our survival strategies for keeping our belongings safe was using a dog crate that we kept strapped to the roof of our van with a tarp taped around it. We would take it down each time we set up camp. It had a lock and we would take our chances by leaving it as we ventured to classes each day. The process of constantly packing and unpacking our stuff caused much anxiety and distress. We shifted our belongings so much that things became broken, worn, and dirty quickly, and our bodies were no different.

There was little time to do homework. And finding Wi-Fi in the places we camped at was nearly impossible at times; this made succeeding in school difficult at best. My grade in world religions dropped because I could not access the resources I needed for a test. We constantly had to charge our electronic devices in our van. We used a solar panel to recharge when we drained its battery. This eventually ruined our electrical system and after nearly 3 months of living rough, we had to invest in a new vehicle. We had no idea at that point how to afford another car. We knew that if we did not have a car, we would not have been able to survive. It provided access to social services, school, HeadStart for my daughter, camping, groceries, and so much more than I could begin to describe. We lucked out with a local dealership. My partner had a relationship with the salesman, and I had good credit. The down payment was deferred for a month until I received my financial aid and student loans.

Without access to a kitchen, my family often had to eat fast food. It's unhealthy and costly. Our county has elected not to offer the California Restaurant Meals Program (RMP), which is the hot food allowance for Supplemental Nutrition Assistance Program (SNAP) eligible households. SNAP was formerly referred to as "food stamps" and in California is named CalFresh. RMP allows eligible homeless, disabled, and/or elderly (ages 60 and above) CalFresh benefit recipients to use their CalFresh benefits to purchase hot, prepared food from participating restaurants. When a household has nowhere to cook or store food safely, this option can really make a difference.

I preferred camping over staying at hotels. In the hotels we sat there in a miserable room. At the camp, it felt like it was home. Our family had more agency, especially with options for cooking and food. At least at the campsites, we could pack up the cooler with veggies from the farmers market that honored our CalFresh and Women, Infants, and Children Food and Nutrition Service (WIC) benefits and fresh meat from the grocery store. It was a chore trying to keep all the food fresh, but I took great care and pride in being able to do it. Wasted food is yet another overwhelming hidden cost of being homeless.

Camping, we kept our kitchen in a suitcase. On a single-burner stove or a beautiful campfire I created my outdoor cooking masterpieces. Each evening, when our family got "home," my love would take our daughter for a walk on the trail, I would take the broom and sweep the redwood needles away from the fire pit, collecting them for kindling. Living without a home, I did the best I could to pretend it is all just normal. As the feast simmered, I would start some housekeeping. I had a tub for dirty dishes, a trash bag, and my towels. Fire-lit family meals with shooting stars holding our dreams. My partner was a great teammate, and I think that acting out these homely steps made it just a little bit easier to feel like family. I mean, for me, as long as I had my belongings, my daughter, my man, and my dogs . . . well, everything was going to be okay! Right!? Too bad we had to move every 7 days from the camp!

I am still paying interest on student loans for the time I was earning a bachelor's degree in sociology and being homeless. In reality, I believe having to survive without a home for so long tore my little family apart literally. Just because we became housed did not mean we healed. It took 2 years to come off of social services, pay the van off, and become housing stable. Eventually, the pain and suffering of an experience like this turns into lifelong trauma and passes down through generations from parents like me and my daughter's father. I can only hope that the education I have fought so vehemently for will ease my daughter's experience of this world. And that it will help raise awareness so that others in my community might be able to heal too.

CATEGORIES OF HOUSING STATUS IN THE CONTINUUM

Housing insecurity involves a range of different residential situations. Researchers, policymakers, and advocates often divide housing insecurity into two groups: homelessness and housing insecurity. While there is significant overlap in the experiences of students in these two groups, understanding the distinctions between categories will enable you to interpret research findings as well as help you think more critically about how to develop supports on your campus.

Housing insecurity involves economic crisis or necessity. A student who chooses to sleep on a friend's couch because they are traveling is not homeless. Similarly, a couple who invites grandparents to live with them for cultural reasons or to assist with childrearing is not housing insecure. Individuals experiencing homelessness and housing insecurity live in unstable housing arrangements because they have no viable alternatives. Homelessness and housing insecurity involve the unplanned loss of housing. Unlike a student with a residence hall contract that ends in May who plans to stay in their parents' home over the summer, unplanned housing insecurity involves uncertainty about how to resolve the issue and may happen with little notice. This will become clear as you read the illustrations threaded throughout this chapter.

Homelessness

A student experiencing homelessness lacks housing that is fixed, regular, and adequate. This language comes from the U.S. Department of Education's definition of homelessness that frames policies related to preschool through high school. Although the McKinney–Vento Homeless Assistance Act, which was reauthorized as part of the Every Student Succeeds Act (2015), outlines educational rights and protections for students in primary and secondary schools, the federal government has yet to create a policy that directly and fully addresses the educational needs of college students experiencing homelessness. We discuss this further in Chapter 3.

At this point it is important to know that our approach to defining *homelessness* has a long history related to policy, practice, advocacy, and research. Our definition reflects an inclusive approach to identifying and explaining homelessness. The U.S. Department of Housing and Urban Development (HUD) more narrowly defines homelessness. HUD focuses on chronic homelessness with particular attention to those living on the streets or in shelters. Given the population often served by HUD, its programs focus on supports related to substance abuse, mental illness, and veteran services. Although HUD officials recognize their definitional approach does not capture a large percentage of the homeless population, they strategically focus on chronic homelessness due to limited financial resources. In addition, they often feel pressure to address the most visible forms of homelessness. Educators and administrators have long understood how this narrow approach inadequately explains student experiences.

Homelessness occurs in many different ways. We recognize that no discussion of homelessness could possibly identify every iteration that exists. Instead of thinking about the following discussion as a comprehensive list, we encourage you to consider the underlying concepts of lacking a fixed, regular, and adequate residence. Students on your campus may have additional situations that would qualify as homeless under that definition. We discuss here seven common forms of homelessness among college students.

Public space. Individuals living in public spaces can take many different forms. In urban areas, you may see people living on the streets, in parks, or near highways. In more rural areas, individuals may seek shelter at local campgrounds, in the woods, in barns and outbuildings, or near rivers and beaches. In some areas small communities may emerge of individuals living in "tent cities" or within an abandoned building. Students may also find refuge on or near the college campus.

Students living in public spaces likely have little access to consistent electricity that would be needed for a computer, alarm clock, or phone. They often have to find campus facilities to heat food or rely on nonperishable food. They likely do not have protection from the weather, which influences their health as well as their ability to keep papers, books, and electronics dry. And the public nature of their living means they have difficulty locking up their valuables, including personal items, schoolbooks, and electronics. Students living in public spaces are also vulnerable to harassment or violent attack. These students may need to bring many of their valuables with them to class or get assistance finding a safe place to store them. In addition, they probably need help accessing a place to shower. Max told us about sleeping on a park bench for months in his first semester in community college.

Max Exits Foster Care

Max emigrated from Iran with his family when he was a small child. When we spoke with him, he was in his second year at a community college. His father was often violent when he was young. Max and his brother were separated from their parents by child protective services when he was a teenager. When Max left the child welfare system at 18, he became a student at a community college, and he also became homeless.

He lived in a park near campus and spoke about how cold it was at night and in the early morning. He explained, "It's like there were some nights where it was unbelievably cold. I literally had to do pushups and jumping jacks and just keep warm. My fingers and my toes were frozen even in my shoes. It was just ridiculous. It was like I stretched out my shirt just trying to keep warm. The next morning I'd just wake up and didn't get any sleep and just hop on the bus and go to school."

Location not intended for human habitation. You may have students taking refuge in places not meant for human habitation. They may be living in abandoned buildings or barns. Some may be renting a shed, garage, or storage unit because they cannot afford the costs of an apartment. We encountered four women in their early 20s who rented a garage from an individual they found on Craigslist. They had a protected space, but no access to a bathroom or kitchen. These students felt fortunate to have protection from the weather and a safe place to store their valuables, which enabled them to feel comfortable leaving for the day to attend classes. They hoped to eventually be able to afford an apartment, but felt lucky they had come across this opportunity that cost about a third of the rate of a two-bedroom apartment.

These locations vary greatly. Some individuals have an agreement with the owner of the building, which may give them access to a key and the ability to lock up their valuables. Others may be staying in the location without permission. Either way, the fact that it is not designed for human habitation means that these spaces may not be safe or healthy places to live and students could be kicked out at any time without notice. The person who owns the location could change the locks and confiscate the students' possessions. The lack of a legal rental agreement makes these locations unstable. The students have limited legal protections and may need assistance accessing legal services if an issue arises. In addition, although these places may give students protection from the weather and even a secure place for personal safety, students may not have access to electricity, a kitchen to store and prepare food, or a bathroom or shower facilities.

Vehicle. Individuals living in vehicles generally need to move frequently to avoid tickets, arrests, and interruptions in the middle of the night. Sleeping in a car has a similar level of public surveillance and risk as living in parks or on the streets. In addition, cities may have laws prohibiting sleeping in a vehicle or parking a camper on the street. Finding a safe and private location each night can be challenging. One student who lived in her car spoke about parking near her high school. She was familiar with the area and felt a sense of safety there. One night, she woke up surrounded by police who were shining a light in her window and yelling to her to step out of the car. She felt afraid for her safety and worried she would be arrested. The officers told her that she could not sleep in that area and she moved on, but she was still anxious when she told us about the incident that had happened the year before.

Sleeping in a car can also be quite challenging since cars are rarely designed with enough space for an adult to lie down. For those individuals sharing a car with another adult or a parent sharing with children, the ability to fully relax and rest is challenging. Students living in vehicles probably do not have consistent access to a bathroom or shower. They have a location to store their valuables, but that space is limited. A trade-off emerges wherein the more space used for storage results in less space for sleep and relaxation. And storing valuables in plain sight can increase the risk that their car may be stolen or broken into and their possessions taken. These students also tend to have limited access to electricity or the Internet.

We should note that individuals living in a camper or house trailer with a consistent rental agreement in a trailer park would not be considered homeless. Generally speaking, these more stable arrangements would be considered fixed, regular, and adequate housing. Unless something occurs that undermines those guidelines, these arrangements would be considered stable housing.

Shelters. Homeless shelters provide a place for individuals to stay for a period of time as well as access to bathrooms and showers. Often these programs offer some level of access to food and/or a kitchen. However, the structure and mission of each shelter influences who qualifies for assistance and how they experience their stay. Each institution has rules that govern the activities of the residents. Transitional-age youth shelters are available for those who are 18 to 24 years old, but not all communities have these forms of support. Adult shelters are often focused on providing services for older adults who may be chronically homeless. Unfortunately, most cities have significantly fewer spaces available in homeless shelters than would be required to meet the need. As a result, your students may be competing with many other individuals for finite resources. To understand the varied nature of homeless shelters, we provide a brief summary of some of the differing formations.

Emergency shelters provide immediate relief. Individuals do not need to apply for assistance. They receive a place to sleep, food, and access to a shower. However, they generally cannot reserve a space for more than one night at a time, and there may be a long line each day. Once capacity is reached, other individuals seeking support are turned away. This means that individuals wanting a place to stay need to start lining up each afternoon, which influences their ability to attend classes, utilize campus resources, and retain evening employment. Many of these shelters utilize dormitory-style sleeping arrangements with large numbers of individuals in one space. The men and women generally get placed in separate spaces or shelters, with boys under a certain age staying with women. The separation of individuals by sex can provide some level of protection against sexual assault, but creates a host of challenges for couples, families, and transgender individuals. Some of these shelters have designated areas for elementary and primary students to study. However, they rarely have space or supports for college students. The goal of these shelters is to provide immediate assistance instead of long-term support.

Many students avoid shelters unless no other option exists. However, Araceli described living in a shelter as better than living on the street, but difficult and stressful. There were rules about what time she had access to her bed and strict guidelines about when lights were turned off for the night. She worried about her items getting stolen, and her place in the shelter was not guaranteed.

Araceli's Experience Living in a Shelter

Araceli, who identified as Filipina, was living in a shelter, working part-time, and attending community college full-time when she was 20 years old. She was grateful to have a place to stay, but she often felt her life was completely out of her control. She said, "I mean like there's a certain time that you need to wake up. There is a certain time that you need to do your chore. You need to somehow meet up [with] your case manager. There are other programs, classes in here that you go [to]. . . . So, yeah, at that time I was really busy."

Transitional shelters provide housing for a certain period of time, often between 3 and 24 months. Some are designated for individuals (generally youth 18 to 24 years old) while others focus on supporting families. A few shelters exist that support LGBTQ+ individuals or those who experienced sex trafficking and/or survival sex (which involves exchanging sex for money, food, or shelter). Transitional shelters often provide small residences, a private room, or a shared apartment. Some include separate kitchen and bathroom facilities for each residence. Individuals need to apply for these programs, and spaces tend to be very limited. Residents get assigned to a case manager who develops a plan that must be followed. For example, most transitional housing programs require the residents to seek employment or education in order to remain in the program. Violation of the transitional plan generally results in loss of housing with little notice.

Many of the students we spoke to in transitional housing were required to focus on employment. A few students lived in programs that had an educational component; however, many students were strongly encouraged to gain employment to establish immediate economic stability and consistency. The students remained conscious that their time in transitional housing was limited. Though they were often working part- or full-time jobs while going to school, they were aware that the stability of transitional living would end. They often sought support from staff to make plans for the program end. At times, they felt pressure to prioritize working more hours in order to prepare for transition out of the program instead of focusing on completing a degree or certificate that may take longer before yielding economic benefits.

Domestic violence shelters provide a refuge most often for women and their children who are escaping abuse. These facilities tend to have a public office where individuals go to see if they qualify for support. However, the living space is in a private location to protect the residents from being located by their abuser. The length of stay varies depending upon the program structure and particulars of the individual case. The residence tends to be a house in a neighborhood with no demarcation that it is a domestic violence shelter. Your students who live in these facilities will generally have access to all the amenities of a home (e.g., Internet, electricity, food, and shower). However, their residential situation is not permanent. And they may have realistic concerns for their safety when coming to campus if their abuser knows about their enrollment. Although the programs take precautions to protect the location of their residents, individuals may need to move on short notice if their abuser finds out their location.

Temporary disaster shelters emerge after a natural or other disaster. This may happen after a hurricane, earthquake, or tornado occurs, or when an apartment building or house burns down. The size of the disaster influences the response. A large disaster may result in the Federal Emergency Management Agency (FEMA) setting up a temporary shelter or utilizing space in community buildings (e.g., churches or schools). Smaller disasters may involve passing out hotel vouchers until individuals can return to their home or make other arrangements. Your students in temporary disaster shelters may have lost clothing, school materials, computers, and other school-related items. They also may be dealing with a number of issues related to housing or rental insurance, health care, and securing new housing. For those using vouchers, they may need to move between different hotels depending upon room availability. Depending on the arrangement, individuals utilizing disaster housing may or may not have access to a kitchen, private bathroom, the Internet, and space to complete homework.

In addition to the basic structure, the mission and funding source of the shelters influence who their residents are and how they serve them. A youth shelter will only allow residents to stay up to a certain age. Generally, youth shelters are for individuals 12–18 or 18–24 years old. These shelters receive funding specifically for those age groups and cannot allow a resident to stay who is outside of that age range without putting their funding in jeopardy. This may separate youth from others with whom they may have developed a connection. Shelters funded by a religious institution may include religious optional or required activities as part of their programming. And, depending on the goals of the shelter, individuals may be encouraged or required to either work or attend school.

Understanding the structure of the shelters around your campus community is important. This enables your institution to create a list of resources available for students. Having a general sense of the program structure allows students to make an informed decision about which program might be the best fit for their particular needs. In addition, your institution may develop outreach and partnerships with the shelters. Often, postsecondary institutions and shelters have little interaction. The differing structures of the shelter and college may make it difficult for students trying to navigate both of the institutions. Many of students living in shelters will qualify for federal and state education grants as well as income-based scholarships. However, they may need assistance in navigating other barriers related to attending school while living in a shelter.

Hotel/motel. Individuals living in a hotel or motel generally have access to a private space and bathroom facilities, but rarely a kitchen or living space. Do not think of the hotels utilized for conferences or vacations. Most individuals living in low-income hotels and motels have minimal space and lack amenities. No one is coming to clean the room each day. Often called welfare hotels, these businesses cater to individuals in poverty. As such, generally all the rooms are rented to individuals by the week or the month. The spaces may

USEFUL RESOURCE: 211

Many communities have a 211 number and website that provides information about services available in your local area. Individuals can speak with a representative who asks for some information about their specific issues and needs. Based upon that short assessment, the individual will be connected with resources. For example, the representative may determine that the call qualifies for emergency housing and can provide information about what shelters have space that night. Individuals can also call 211 when they need information about mental health, addiction support, and other social services.

While you could call to get general information about what may be available to address an issue, the person needing support will have to be on the phone to receive specific recommendations. However, you may want to help initiate the call and be available to encourage the student to move forward with accessing the services.

be less expensive than an apartment, but also have significantly less space. Some of the buildings require individuals to share a communal bathroom.

While your students staying in a hotel may have a private space that can be secured, they may find it difficult to study in the crowded space. In addition, they may have limited access to the Internet. Individuals living in hotels also do not have a long-term contract. The rental agreements may be night-to-night, week-to-week, or one month at a time. At any point, the hotel manager can ask a resident to leave with little or no notice. The residents have little, if any, legal grounds to dispute a notice that their contract will not be extended. That being said, students in these situations should be referred to legal housing support if they believe their contract has been unfairly terminated.

Couch or dorm surfing. Individuals who couch surf lack the stability of knowing where they will stay each night. Some practitioners and policymakers argue this is not homelessness because the students may be doing this for adventure or a carefree lifestyle. They attribute this living arrangement to traveling around Europe and staying in hostels. While this may happen with some students, we reject the idea that all couch surfing is a choice. Remember the clarification above that these living arrangements must be a result of economic necessity or crisis. Your students who are couch surfing because they have no alternative options are not doing so out of a sense of adventure. They are homeless and trying to survive. And their living arrangements create educational challenges as well as significant emotional stress.

A person who is couch surfing often has to develop relationships with multiple individuals who may be willing to allow them to stay for a short period of time—sometimes relocating to a different person's house every night. Students who sleep in the dorm rooms of their peers who are living in campus housing have a similar experience to those who are sleeping on the couches of independent adults. However, students who sleep as unpaid guests in dorms have an additional dilemma. The student who is extending this opportunity can be evicted from housing if they are violating the rules of their residence hall contracts. Choosing between sleeping in a car or sleeping in a dorm room putting their friends at risk of eviction causes stress, guilt, and strain on their relationships.

Your students who couch surf may have little certainty of where they will stay each night. This means that part of each day involves dedicating time and energy to figuring out where they will sleep. They also need to move their belongings each day. They may move around to different parts of the city or surrounding cities frequently, which can create issues related to transportation to and from school if they do not have a car. In addition, they may be worried about damaging relationships that not only provide emotional support and connection, but also serve as important resources for short-term housing. As a result, students who are couch surfing often need to keep a detailed account of where they have stayed in order to avoid asking too much of one individual that could result in that relationship ending. Hailey's experiences illustrate the relational and emotional stress created by couch surfing.

Hailey's Experience of Couch Surfing

At 18 years old, Hailey spoke to us about living place-to-place with friends. She had not identified a major at the time and was trying to complete her general education courses. Hailey was a former foster youth and had little contact with her biological or foster families. She spoke about anxiety of not knowing where she was going to sleep each night and the tension that was created in her college life when she was living with friends, but also trying not to wear out her welcome. She made a policy not to stay longer than 3 days at any one location.

"Like, everybody's going home [from class], and it's like, hey dude, can I crash at your pad? Like, ahhh, you get so frustrated like, just to be asking people for a place to stay, like, after a while . . . like, there is a saying in Spanish, 'The dead cat stinks at 3 days' . . . like you can't stay in the same house for more than 3 days."

Housing Instability

Unstable housing situations are those that may not remain fixed, regular, and adequate. These students may have a current place to live, but that circumstance could come to an end in the near future. Students living in residence halls on campus who do not have a place to live during breaks or after graduation would fit into this category. For example, we worked with a student who lived in a residence hall during the semester and stayed with her mother in an emergency homeless shelter during winter break. Students who are unable to fulfill their residence hall payment plan could fall into this category if they have nowhere else to live.

Students may also be living off campus in residential situations that are unstable. They may be a month or more behind on rent. This situation could also occur when a roommate is behind on rent or moves out with little notice. Your students may be going through foreclosure or eviction. When current housing comes to an end and the students do not have viable housing as a result of limited resources, they would be considered unstably housed due to economic crises. One student recounted repeatedly getting 3-day eviction notices because their landlord was strategizing to raise their rent. These examples of ongoing risk of homelessness creates feelings of stress and anxiety.

Doubled-up residences would also be considered unstable housing. *Doubled-up residences* are when two or more families are living in a space designed for one as a result of economic necessity. This does not mean that every roommate situation would be considered unstably housed. Two individuals renting a two-bedroom apartment would be stably housed. Most college students between 18 and 24 years of age live in this sort of arrangement at some point.

Unstable housing can also involve situations where individuals are making decisions about paying rent or utility bills and purchasing food. Many students talk about experiences with food insecurity, having diminished in quality or nutrition of food or skipping meals, while homeless. Students described often living paycheck to paycheck, using credit cards to pay bills, or becoming delinquent in bill payment while waiting for financial aid disbursements.

Recent Housing Instability

Many definitions focus on a binary: homeless and not homeless. We strongly encourage you to think in terms of a continuum, which more accurately reflects students' experiences. An important aspect of that continuum involves students who are currently housed, but have a recent history of housing instability. While their current housing needs may be addressed, they may have residual effects related to the traumas associated with housing instability and homelessness.

Students with recent housing instability have secured stability, but have had a recent history of housing instability within the past 3 years. These individuals may or may not need continued support. While their housing needs may be addressed, they may have continued challenges associated with their previous residential experiences. Researchers have found that losing housing security can create a fear that it may happen again (Barker, 2016). Students who have experienced loss of housing may come to believe that any housing situation is temporary, which can lead to self-sabotaging behaviors. We have worked with students who have been living in "survival mode" for so long that, once they find housing stability, they experience anxiety, depression, or other emotional and psychological responses that they have been suppressing while responding to crisis. They may feel worse physically or mentally, because they have the mental capacity to rest long enough to think about what they have endured. As a result, the transition to housing should include counseling and other supports.

When Financial Aid Is Not Enough

Tony was awarded scholarships and financial aid that fully funded his expenses for his education, his basic needs, and a little more for his personal life; however, his history with insecurity followed him into college. He often stocked up food or money, skipping meals and lapsing bills, because he feared that his newfound stability might disappear. Although Tony achieved residential stability, he continued to experience the emotional impacts of his experiences with homelessness.

Housing Security

Housing security exists when individuals have consistent access to fixed, adequate, and safe housing with reliable funding to cover expenses. Many students who share an apartment off campus with a roommate would be housing secure if they have a consistent way to pay for rent, utilities, and food. Similarly, a student living with a partner and their child in a two-bedroom house with adequate means to cover basic needs would also be considered secure. Just as there are many ways that an individual can experience homelessness and housing insecurity, there are also multiple living arrangements that would be considered housing secure.

In addition to the residential arrangements, students that are housing secure have other important characteristics. These individuals generally have social connections and a safety net. Their social networks include friends, family, colleagues, and partners with stable housing. If a financial issue should emerge, these students could reach out to someone in their social network. Particularly, for seemingly minor financial issues (e.g., being short $100 for rent or an unexpected cost for school), these individuals would have people who could assist in covering the cost. Their social network can prevent a "small" financial issue from becoming a crisis that results in loss of housing and dropping out of school. Their relationships may also be important when a major financial issue emerges (e.g., losing a job or divorce).

Even strong networks of support often have limitations. At some point, friends and family may feel the costs of the relationship are too high and they expect the individuals to figure out how to fix their financial issues on their own. The combination of lacking personal resources as well as draining social network support generally leads to housing insecurity.

PERSON-FIRST LANGUAGE

You may have noticed that we avoid terms like *homeless person* or *the homeless*. We recommend employing person-first language that prioritizes a positive and empowering identity—student—instead of a socially stigmatized situation (e.g., student experiencing housing insecurity). This is more than semantics. Individuals unable to meet basic needs experience social shame in the United States. Anchoring their identity primarily in a stigmatized situation may have negative psychological impacts as well as reducing the likelihood that they will utilize services. Having a "homeless student club" would probably be ineffective because few students will want to be associated with that identity, especially in a public forum. Similarly, programs for "the needy" or "needy students" may result in low participation.

The stigma associated with homelessness and basic needs insecurity also means you should be cautious about how you employ the terms when designing services on campus. A contradictory context exists. Individuals may avoid programs associated with homelessness, but they also will have a difficult time finding the supports if the programs are vaguely identified. We discuss program development further in the chapters that follow. At this point, we want to suggest employing descriptive and inclusive language when discussing the issue with students. Having a "housing support program" with a description of situations that may fit within that the program of support is one way to avoid making students identify with the term *homeless*. At the same time, you will want to include keywords such as *homeless* and *hunger* within the text of the resource page and in the page's metadata so that students searching for resources using those terms can still find the page.

CONCLUSION

College students experience housing insecurity in a variety of ways. The general uncertainty about residential stability is a common trait. However, each residential situation involves different challenges. A one-size-fits-all approach would be inadequate. Throughout the remaining chapters, we provide guidance in exploring different ways to design supports for your students.

Application on Your Campus

- Create campus training and resources designed to help faculty, administration, professionals, students, and support personnel understand what homelessness and housing insecurity look like using the definitional continuum provided in this chapter. This is an important first step. Individuals on campus need a clear sense of the issues in order to move toward identifying and implementing supports.
- Engage in conversations and exploration to uncover the different ways that homelessness and housing insecurity exist among students on your campus. Ask staff, faculty, and administrators about examples they might have working with or teaching students who have experienced homelessness and housing instability.
- Locate and contact local agencies and advocates to understand groups of individuals who attend your institution as well as those who want to attend your institution, but face barriers due to housing insecurity.

CHAPTER 3

Social and Political Context

Homelessness and housing insecurity are not isolated issues. Lack of stable housing is a symptom of issues in an individual's life that are created, influenced, or exacerbated by societal challenges. This may seem counterintuitive, but housing insecurity is not just a housing issue. The reasons why a person lives without stability are important to consider. As we discuss further in the remaining chapters, a trauma-informed approach requires understanding and addressing the underlying issues related to housing insecurity.

Broadly speaking, social and political contexts frame both why a person becomes housing insecure and how they experience it. A holistic approach to understanding housing insecurity reveals the complex social, political, and personal issues that result in an individual living without stable housing. Since higher education institutions generally consider themselves as serving the local community, positioning your institution to understand and address housing insecurity can be an important service to the long-term economic success of the state and nation.

ECONOMIC CONTEXT

The United States has seen unemployment rates decline in recent years. The broad view of the economic conditions seems to suggest that individuals are financially thriving, but there is also healthy skepticism concerning the fragility of the economy and unequal distribution of financial benefit between the highest and lowest economic brackets. Some individuals have benefited from the economic growth since the Great Recession. However, a more nuanced view is needed to understand why students pursing higher education experience financial challenges that result in food and housing insecurity.

Postsecondary Costs

The cost of attending postsecondary institutions has steadily increased since 2008. Most states across the nation reduced funding to state colleges and universities at the start of the Great Recession. Even during the period of economic recovery and growth, federal and state governments have de-invested in higher education (Goldrick-Rab, 2016; Newfield, 2018). Although the actual cost of running a postsecondary institution has not significantly risen in the past decade, a shift of college costs has moved from the states to the students. The long-term economic success of the states and nation directly relate to having an educated workforce, but short-term political benefits of reducing taxes and moving funding in other directions often motivates elected officials to decrease higher education funding. As a result, the tuition and fees students pay dramatically increased each year since 2008.

Unfortunately, the state and federal grants designed to support college students with financial need have not kept pace with the increased cost of attendance. For example, the federal Pell Grant covered the entire costs of attending a community college when it was first created; however, now it only covers about 60% of community college tuition and fees and less than half of the cost of attending a 4-year institution (Goldrick-Rab et al., 2015; U.S. Department of Housing and Urban Development [HUD], 2015). Whereas students from low-income backgrounds could attend a postsecondary institution with little or no loan debt a few decades ago, the reduced relative value of federal and state grants currently results in many students acquiring significant student loan debt. In addition to tuition costs, housing and living expenses have become a larger proportion of college costs than was the case when the Pell Grant was created (Goldrick-Rab et al., 2015). For most students attending a 4-year institution, housing and living expenses now account for about half of the cost of attendance (HUD, 2015).

Housing Costs

The cost of housing in the United States has continued to rise. A person working a full-time minimum wage job cannot afford to rent a house, purchase food, and cover modest personal expenses in most cities across the nation. An increasing number of families and individuals live in doubled-up residences, meaning that a space designed for one family is being shared by two or more families as a result of economic crises (Hallett, 2012).

Costs of on-campus housing options have also risen during this time. In addition to the increased expenses of building and maintaining housing units, many college campuses with residence halls have also responded to their students' requests for on-campus housing with more space and amenities. In place of the lower-cost traditional residence hall studio-style rooms with two to four students, many postsecondary institutions have felt pressure to create apartment-style suites in order to compete for students. While these accommodations can be more comfortable for the students and may improve the likelihood of building a sense of community, they also cost significantly more than studio-style rooms to build and maintain. Many universities now have room and board costs that are significantly higher than tuition and fees. Some students may be able to secure money and aid to cover the costs of tuition, but be unable to consistently do so for the cost of housing.

In addition to the rental and mortgage costs associated with housing, individuals generally have utilities as added housing expenses. As an indirect housing cost, utilities can be a significant cost for students. If not paid, a shutoff can lead to associated life consequences (e.g., no lights, heating, refrigeration for food, Internet access, and power source for computer, phone, and health support technology). When utilities get discontinued, there may be incurred fees and back payment required before they will be reinstated as well as increased deposit requirements.

Your students who do not have consistent financial support to cover costs of housing, food, and utilities may be forced to make difficult decisions about how to use their limited resources. Do they pay rent and sacrifice access to food or utilities? Or do they choose an unstable or inadequate housing option in order to eat regularly? Do they drop out of school in order to work a second part-time job that may allow for short-term financial resources, but limits their long-term economic stability? Unfortunately, some of your students may also consider engaging in dangerous behaviors. For example, we spoke with a female student who regularly used dating apps and online chat rooms to find men to purchase her meals. A few times, she ended up in situations that felt dangerous. In order to fully understand your students' financial stress, you should engage in a thoughtful exploration of the multiple expenses beyond tuition.

SOCIAL CONTEXT

Housing insecurity correlates with many other social issues. In many ways, basic needs insecurity tends to be a symptom of personal and societal issues. We have not encountered a situation where everything else is going well in students' lives, but they lack resources to consistently access food and housing. Rather, the challenges in students' lives are typically coupled with societal inequities or personal crises leading to loss of stable housing. Individuals marginalized by society are particularly vulnerable to homelessness and housing insecurity. We explore here a few of the more common issues that relate to housing insecurity for college students.

Individuals who have been in the foster care system experience increased likelihood of experiencing homelessness and housing insecurity as adults. Advocates and social services agencies have worked to develop transition plans for individuals as they transition out of foster care. In addition, these individuals get priority access to most state and federal grants for higher education. Some states, like California, have specific grants for former foster youth to assist with the costs of postsecondary education. However, their lack of social and familial networks continues to put them at risk for housing insecurity.

The LGBTQ+ community experiences disproportionately high rates of homelessness and housing insecurity. Some of your students who grow up in middle- or upper-class communities may experience familial and social rejection when their LGBTQ+ identity is revealed. In these situations, the individual often has no experience with how to access support from social services. Your students may experience this situation prior to entering college or during their academic careers.

The United States has a long history of racial discrimination, which results in inequitable opportunities. Racially minoritized groups experience housing insecurity as college students more often than their White peers. In particular, African American, Southeast Asian, and multiracial students have relatively higher rates of housing insecurity (Wood et al., 2017).

Students attending college who are over the age of 25 also have higher rates of homelessness than their peers who are 18–22 years old (Tsui et al., 2011; Wood et al., 2017). Similarly, students who are parenting are more likely than their nonparenting peers to experience housing insecurity (Tsui et al., 2011).

People without housing security may also have limited access to health care, including counseling services. A student in higher education may be deemed ineligible for social services. A personal health crisis can disrupt a person's housing situation, leading someone who had been housed to become homeless. Homelessness and housing insecurity also correlate with multiple forms of abuse, including physical, sexual, and substance abuse.

We encourage considering an intersectional approach when exploring the issue of basic needs insecurity. For example, you may be working with a White woman over the age of 25 who has children and works while attending school, but makes below a living wage. Or you may have a gay Southeast Asian man who recently graduated from high school, but is independent of parental assistance. We address this not to participate in "oppression Olympics," measuring the value of layered marginalization, but rather because intersectionality explores how overlapping and interlocking social oppression may further complicate a student's ability to secure stable housing. Increasing college access and retention for these students can be particularly important in helping them achieve long-term housing stability.

While the social context is important to consider, we want to emphasize that students experiencing homelessness and housing insecurity are quite similar to their peers. They have goals and ambitions. They experience success and failure in college. The key difference tends to be the limited personal safety net when a crisis emerges. Being aware of the social conditions is important and may help programs target specific interventions based upon the specific group of students served, but we strongly discourage essentializing students. Each student brings different strengths and challenges that warrant consideration as you develop a plan for their success.

We share this information to underscore the importance of collaborating with programs, services, and organizations across campus. Your campus likely has programming and student groups related to the social issues discussed above. We encourage you to collaborate with these groups in order to more fully understand the issue as well as during the implementation process. We also recommend using the information about social inequities to understand the general context of homelessness and housing insecurity, but focus support efforts on meeting the individual needs of students. Each student has unique experiences and needs. Not all students with a marginalized identity will necessarily be at risk of housing insecurity. The California State University (CSU) Study of Student Basic Needs illustrates the social context of homelessness and housing insecurity among college students.

Equity and Impact on Education

In the CSU Study of Student Basic Needs (Crutchfield & Maguire, 2018, 2019), we found overrepresentation of multiple groups of students in prevalence numbers for experiences of homelessness (e.g., former foster youth, LGBTQ+, first-generation college students). Also, some groups of students of color largely reported experiencing more barriers to accessing services on campus than Asian and/or White students, which is an additional issue related to equity.

Disparities among demographics were clearer when the intersection of first-generation college students and race/ethnicity were examined. Students who identified as Black/African American and first-generation college students (18%) experienced homelessness at much higher rates than any other racial or ethnic group who were also the first in their family to attend college (9.6–12.6%). In addition, students who were former foster youth (24.9%) had more than double the average CSU rate of homelessness (10.9%).

Housing insecurity directly impacts students. We found that meeting basic needs often generated stress for students, exacerbating challenges to their physical and mental health. Students who were food insecure, homeless, or both reported symptoms of poor physical and mental health leading to more missed days of work or school in the past 30 days than students who were food secure or housed.

Students who reported very low food security in the past 30 days missed between 7 and 8 days of work or school in the past 30 days because of poor mental and/or physical health symptoms compared with 2–3 missed days for students reporting high food security. Students who reported being homeless one or more times in the past 12 months reported missing between 6 and 8 days of school or work in the past 30 days, compared with 4–5 days of missed work or school for students who did not report any incidents of homelessness in the past 12 months.

IMPACT ON EDUCATION

Basic needs insecurity influences how students experience higher education. Researchers have found that students who reported housing insecurity or homelessness also experienced negative physical and mental health consequences. Students described how experiencing housing insecurity influenced most facets of life, including academic struggle, long work hours, and negative impact on mental and physical health. Despite this, many attempt to persist until graduation. Often, students who lack basic needs have lower academic achievement. Participating in their usual activities associated with school, work, self-care, and recreation can be undermined because of physical and mental distress.

Many students talk about feeling isolated from their peers for a variety of reasons. Some students may rely on peers for emotional or financial support or for a place to stay. They feel like a drain on their friends and are in a state of constant worry that they will lose those friendships. Other students keep their circumstances secret for fear that if their peers find out about their situation, they will be pitied or rejected. Students decline invitations to study groups and social outings because they cannot afford to contribute to a meal or feel too ashamed to talk about their home lives. Teri spoke about her frustrations about being isolated on campus.

Teri's Experience on Campus

Teri was 20, living in a transitional living facility, and attending her first year of community college when we spoke to her. She could make friends easily, but felt isolated on days she spent on campus. She said, "It's sad, and I don't have friends or anything. In school, I wasn't able to be a social butterfly because I was embarrassed of my situation. I can't really go out. [They'll ask] 'Where do you live? Can we pick you up?' Like, I was really antisocial, and it really took a toll."

When Teri was asked what people should know about her college experiences, she spoke in the third person. She said, "The thing that I really want you to focus on is that it was difficult for her to build relationships because she was embarrassed of her status, homelessness. It was harder for her to reach out too because she was scared. I felt scared. I was intimidated . . . oh my God, I'm so little."

When they are able to participate in regular activities, students who lack food and housing security are often required to spread their time across a wide variety of personal, employment, and educational demands. Students who experience both homelessness and food insecurity are most likely to be employed for pay at the highest number of hours per week allowed compared with their basic needs–secure peers (Crutchfield & Maguire, 2019).

Individuals experiencing homelessness and housing insecurity often also have inconsistent access to food. Lacking food security further complicates your students' ability to fully academically engage in classes and assignments. Many students who experience food insecurity, homelessness, or both have lower grade point averages (GPAs) than those who are basic needs secure. Findings in studies on collegiate homelessness in California (Crutchfield & Maguire, 2018) show that students who report food insecurity and homelessness experience adverse effects on their physical and mental health.

Trying to Make Food Last

We have spoken with many students who have to make food stretch to ensure that they have something to eat throughout the day every day. Susan spoke both about the stress to make food last and how this influenced her ability to function academically. She said, "I would get bananas and I will cut it in half. I'd eat only half in the morning, and then I would wait 5 hours, then eat the other half, just so I have something in my stomach consistently. . . . I would struggle to concentrate [in school] for sure, because sometimes that's all I could think about, where was my next meal going to come from."

Many students report that they have the academic skill to achieve, but housing instability negatively impacts their GPAs. Students talk about having to sacrifice time for coursework to find places to stay, or experience stress and anxiety that make it difficult to concentrate while studying. Many students that we have worked with have emphasized how difficult it can be to persistently think about or seek a place to stay. It can be "like a job," and causes stress, anxiety, lack of focus, and difficulty finding time and locations to study in a quiet place.

Surprisingly, other students who experienced homelessness report high overall GPAs because they spend long hours on campus as a safe place to rest (Crutchfield & Maguire, 2018). Many students experiencing homelessness arrive to campus early in the morning and stay until the evening in order to find refuge. They spend long hours in the library and other common spaces on campus because they have no other place to go. They may have high grades because they spend so much time studying in what for other students might be social or recreational time.

Unfortunately, these high grades come at a steep cost. Students who are food insecure, homeless, or both report poorer physical and mental health than their secure peers (Crutchfield & Maguire, 2018). Students report high levels of personal concerns like anxiety, fear, irritability, and depression. They discuss working multiple jobs to make ends meet while also taking courses and trying to find food and shelter. They can feel nauseous, dizzy, or unwell overall.

Running Out of Energy

Priscilla, who identified as Latina, was 20 years old and majoring in art as a junior at a 4-year university when she spoke with us. She told us, "I would save money and get the cheapest foods and I started feeling really lethargic, just nasty, you don't get the energy. . . . We have this whole focus, this whole responsibility on our shoulders."

POLICIES FRAMING HIGHER EDUCATION

For many policymakers and practitioners, the experience of college is one of change, transition, and exploration. Nostalgic memories of college often include managing a personal budget for the first time, sometimes resulting in making poor financial decisions that led their parents to restrict how much money they could get for social engagement. We have heard people talk about how they "had to eat cups of noodles too" when they mismanaged money. We agree that college can be a good time to test out skills needed for adulthood. However, the students we are talking about face obstacles that many policymakers and practitioners cannot imagine. Shifting the narrative about what basic needs insecurity means is an important component of building policies to support students.

Unlike the preschool through high school systems, a comprehensive federal policy has not been developed to specifically address the issue of homelessness and housing insecurity in higher education. However, policy signals in the Every Student Succeeds Act of 2015 (ESSA) and other laws suggest that the federal government may move in that direction at some point. To understand the current policy environment, we review policies that currently provide some guidance for postsecondary institutions: McKinney–Vento Act, College Cost Reduction and Access Act (2007), and Every Student Succeeds Act (2015). We also explore state-level policies that offer support for college students experiencing housing or food insecurity. Understanding key public policies that shape housing security for college students is essential for higher education administrators. The policies offer resources and constraints for improving safe and affordable student housing options. In the sections that follow, we provide an overview of the policies as they influence postsecondary education. (For a full review of the federal policies in terms of the implications for K–12 education, please refer to *Serving Students Who Are Homeless* by Hallett & Skrla, 2017.)

McKinney-Vento Homeless Assistance Act

The McKinney–Vento Act, which was reauthorized in 2015, primarily focuses on preschool through high school education. The law creates rights for families and students experiencing homelessness, including the ability to enroll without delay and access to transportation to school even when they move outside of school boundaries (Miller, 2011a, 2011b; Pavlakis, 2014). The McKinney–Vento Act has been revised multiple times since 1987. Each round of revision further defined and increased protections for students and families. The policy has generally been bipartisan with the act being signed by President Reagan and significant revisions signed by Presidents Clinton, G. W. Bush, and Obama.

The McKinney–Vento Act primarily has indirect influences on higher education and serves as a policy signal of where federal and state policies may be headed. The overarching goal of the federal policy is to identify and remove educational barriers for students who are homeless. States, school districts, and schools are required to review policies and practices to understand the potential negative consequences for students. For example, obtaining a school uniform and school supplies tends to be financially difficult for families who are homeless. As a result, these students must be assisted in securing these items. As Chapter 2 illustrates, the law also has an inclusive approach to homelessness, which frames how the U.S. Department of Education, state governments, and school districts define homelessness.

The College Cost Reduction and Access Act of 2007 (CCRAA) includes a provision to allow unaccompanied students experiencing homelessness to apply for federal financial aid without parental information or signature. The district homeless liaison can sign documentation concerning a student's status, which allows the application to be submitted as an independent student and the postsecondary institution can calculate financial aid with the assumption of no family financial contribution.

For a higher education professional, there are a few other elements within McKinney–Vento that are worth considering. First, the law requires school districts to have a point of contact for students experiencing homelessness in K–12 educational systems. The homeless liaison coordinates services for students and provides training for school site professionals. Students and families can meet with the homeless liaison to get support. The law also encourages schools to work collaboratively with community agencies. To return to the school uniform example, the school could coordinate with a social service agency, community center, or business to provide those items for students. While not explicitly required by federal law, higher education institutions would benefit from having a point of contact who coordinates services on campus as well as collaborating with community agencies. Policy advocates Barbara Duffield and Patricia Julianelle of SchoolHouse Connection share important work they have done with policy advocacy.

The Imperative of Policy Advocacy

Barbara Duffield, *executive director, SchoolHouse Connection*
Patricia Julianelle, *director of program advancement and legal affairs, SchoolHouse Connection*

Higher education offers a means to escape homelessness and poverty permanently, both for young people who experience homelessness today and for their children. As such, higher education is a critical, if often overlooked, element in combatting homelessness. Yet, as this book describes, students who experience homelessness face many barriers in their pursuit of higher education. Some of these barriers are caused by federal and state policies that even the most proactive and informed institution, and the most savvy, creative, and compassionate practitioner, cannot overcome. Thus an effective response to homelessness in higher education necessitates policy advocacy at the federal and state levels.

At SchoolHouse Connection our approach to federal and state policy advocacy is to listen and learn, then advocate and implement. The biggest higher education policy barrier that we have witnessed is access to financial aid—specifically, the requirements for youth under age 24 to have access to parental income information in order to complete the FAFSA. Prior to the enactment of the College Cost Reduction and Access Act of 2007, this requirement posed almost insurmountable barriers to unaccompanied homeless youth, who are extremely poor and who are not supported by their parents. A multiyear advocacy effort involving K–12 McKinney-Vento school district liaisons, homeless service providers, and youth themselves resulted in an amendment to the Higher Education Act (2008) to allow certain parties to verify the homeless and unaccompanied status of youth, and therefore allow them to obtain independent student status.

Thousands of youth have benefited from this amendment; however, much work remains to be done. Youth who are unaccompanied and homeless still face burdensome documentation requirements, both as a result of poor implementation of current law and as a result of limitations in the law itself. Beyond access to federal student aid, additional systemic barriers to retention and success include lack of housing during academic breaks and the academic year, and lack of assistance navigating higher education systems.

The vehicle for federal higher education policy change for youth who are homeless is bipartisan legislation—the proposed Higher Education Access and Success for Homeless and Foster Youth Act (HEASHFY). HEASHFY streamlines the financial aid process for these youth. It also requires colleges and universities to designate higher education liaisons to develop a plan to assist youth to access housing resources during and between academic terms. The 116th Congress is poised to take up the reauthorization of the Higher Education Act, which offers a critical opportunity to advocate for these and other amendments.

State policy reform is an important complementary strategy to advocacy with the U.S. Congress and federal agencies. State college and university systems vary in their methods of governance and administration. Therefore, state laws can be tailored for the particular structure of a state system. In addition, state legislatures often operate more quickly than Congress, allowing advocates to achieve policy changes that help youth access and succeed in higher education immediately, as federal policies work their way through the process. Several states have enacted legislation to reduce barriers to retention and success in higher education for students experiencing homelessness. These laws codify best practices such as tuition waivers, allowances for in-state tuition, housing priorities, higher education liaisons, and priority enrollment to assist homeless and foster youth. In the 2019 legislative sessions the legislatures of Indiana, Maine, Tennessee, and Texas will consider similar bills. SchoolHouse Connection will work with each of these states on their legislative reforms and implementation.

For more resources and updates, please visit www.schoolhouseconnection.org/

Every Student Succeeds Act

The Every Student Succeeds Act of 2015 (ESSA) included a reauthorization of McKinney–Vento. A few important aspects of ESSA pertain to higher education, including college preparation and access. First, homeless liaisons must inform unaccompanied youth who are homeless about their ability to establish independent student status on their Free Application for Federal Student Aid (FAFSA). This has important implications for students. They are to be informed of their rights and given information about how to exercise those rights. Students who have independent status do not need to provide the tax forms of their parents, and their estimated financial contribution to their education is measured solely by their own income. In reality, many unaccompanied students experiencing homelessness would qualify for a similar amount of financial aid even if their parents' incomes were included on the FAFSA because their families likely have limited financial resources. However, removing the requirement for locating family financial records significantly increases the likelihood that students who are unaccompanied can complete the FAFSA forms. For a subset of the unaccompanied student population, the ability to file as an independent allows them access to financial aid even though their family income would typically disqualify them from financial aid. These are individuals who have been kicked out of or have run away from their family's home as a result of abuse. Their families may refuse to provide financial records or it may be dangerous for the student to return to the family residence to request documentation. For example, some young people have been asked to leave their homes after revealing they are LGBTQ+. Sadly, these individuals may have no connection with their family and receive no financial support. The ability to apply as an independent student improves access to financial aid, which increases access to higher education.

ESSA also increased access to extracurricular activities for students in high school. Schools are now required to review policies that limit access to extracurricular activities for students experiencing homelessness. In terms of higher education, this means more students should have access to college preparation programming and extracurricular activities that may increase prospective students' ability to be competitive in the college application process.

Further, ESSA specifically states that federal college access programs, like TRIO, must give priority to students who experience homelessness. On campuses with large populations of low-income students, this is of particular importance since these programs often reach capacity quickly. TRIO and other equal opportunity programs can provide important resources like tutoring, course counseling, social supports, and scholarships, all of which are vital resources for students of limited means.

Of particular importance to higher education, the federal law now considers housing status to be a Family Educational Rights and Privacy Act (FERPA; 1974) issue. Educational professionals should not share the student's status with others. Even on campus, the student's status should only be shared with those individuals who need to know in order to more adequately support the student. For example, the point of contact on campus could reach out to financial aid on behalf of the student in order to resolve an issue. However, they should not post on social media about a student's status or discuss that person's situation with another student. Policy advocate Tanisha Saunders shares her experiences working to influence local, state, and national policies.

Influencing Policy

Tanisha Saunders, *policy and legislative affairs fellow,*
Los Angeles Homeless Services Authority

Prior to transferring to a 4-year university from my community college in the spring of 2016, I was homeless. I was an honors student, a devoted student leader and community member; yet, no one knew I was sleeping in my car. I was in foster care in my adolescence, and as I was entering university, a family member offered me a room to rent. I excitedly accepted the offer, as I also relished the opportunity to build a relationship with my family. Less than a month after our agreement, I was evicted without warning. I reached out to campus housing for assistance, but I'd missed housing deadlines. My family relationships were strained, but I moved in with my mother and stepfather despite my own misgivings. Less than 2 weeks later, my stepfather was murdered. My home wasn't safe, and I started living in my car. My first night sleeping in my car, I awoke to police officers telling me that I had to leave the residential location I was in. I applied for government food assistance but was denied because I was not employed the 20 hours a week required to be eligible as a student.

I spent a large portion of my semester in university trying to secure housing. I was employed in the university library, but I quit when the pressure of the work schedule, the stress of being homeless, and the impacts of trauma began to affect my grades. After several months, I was able to secure housing, a shared one-bedroom apartment 30 miles away from campus. Along my journey of homelessness, I discovered that there were various support systems on campus, such as food pantries and counseling. I also began to see that the California State University system was aware many students faced housing and food insecurity and were working to address the issue. This awareness of students' adversity and concern assured me that I was in the right place and motivated me to be more involved on campus and in the community. I began sharing my story publicly and joined the National Foster Youth Institute (NFYI), an organization that advocates for the transformation of the child welfare system. Homelessness is an issue that disproportionately affects foster youth. As a member of NFYI, I learned advocacy skills while working alongside elected officials and my peers to change the negative outcomes that affect foster youth and families. In the past 2 years, I have had the opportunity to advocate for changes at the local, state, and national level for foster youth and the education system.

I would like for everyone to realize the impact they can have by creating an inclusive and aware environment. We are in school because we believe that education is the gateway to success, and it is imperative that our humanity is affirmed as we fight for what we believe in. The time is now to implement innovative policies that combat food and housing insecurity, that account for the diverse experiences that students at various identity intersections are facing while building a future for themselves. As a poor African American woman and former foster youth, I overcame many obstacles in the pursuit of my bachelor of science degree in child development, which took me 11 years to complete. Throughout my journey, I realized that the different intersections of my identity directly affected the ways in which I struggled and even succeeded throughout my journey. Supportive people and responsive environments allowed me to look beyond my circumstances, power through adversity, and become a community advocate. I am currently a Policy and Legislative Affairs Fellow at the Los Angeles Homeless Services Authority, where I use my lived experience to guide me as I contribute to the work to end homelessness in Los Angeles. In the future, I would like to obtain a master of social work degree and partner with underserved communities to build coalitions rooted in uplifting the cultural, social, and human capital that exists within everyone, while advocating for equity within public institutions.

State Policies

In the absence of a comprehensive federal policy concerning housing insecurity in higher education, some states have created policies to support college students. In particular, California has taken the lead on creating several policies. Even if you do not live in California, several of the laws could be implemented at an institutional level.

State policies have developed in four key areas: housing, enrollment, tuition, and hygiene. In many ways these policies mirror the underlying tenets of the federal policies governing K–12 schools. California and Louisiana give students experiencing homelessness priority access to residence halls. For postsecondary institutions with limited on-campus housing, these policies allow students without alternative housing to secure a room. For campuses with multiple different housing plans, these students may be more likely to get into a residence hall with year-round access. Granted, these laws do not apply to campuses without residence halls.

California also gives students experiencing housing insecurity priority enrollment. Similar to other groups of students that get an early enrollment time (e.g., athletes and former foster youth), students experiencing homelessness get an opportunity to select courses prior to general enrollment. This increases the likelihood they will get into classes that will move them toward graduation as quickly as possible. In addition, the early enrollment allows for these students to build a schedule that works around their housing situation. Shahera Hyatt's work as a policy advocate and researcher has been instrumental in policy development in California.

State-Level Advocacy

Shahera Hyatt, *MSW, director, California Homeless Youth Project*

I dropped out of high school at the age of 16. I was an unlikely candidate to go to college, but that's exactly where I headed after passing the California High School Proficiency Exam. I bounced from friend's house to friend's house, all while knowing that education would be my pathway out of poverty. As a 16-year-old unaccompanied community college student without a stable place to live, navigating the higher education system was a challenge. I wasn't savvy about financial aid and missed out on a lot of support as a result. Since receiving my master's degree in social work from California State University, Sacramento, and becoming the director of the California Homeless Youth Project, I've remained committed to supporting young people in similar situations in order to reduce hardship and promote equity.

In 2015 I began holding focus groups with college students experiencing homelessness. When asked what they needed to be successful in college, their overwhelming response was positive relationships with supportive adults. For me, this answer underscores the fact that many young people experiencing homelessness aren't just suffering from economic poverty, but are also lacking the supportive relationships necessary to succeed in adulthood. Listening to the community most impacted by an issue is key to developing effective policy. The expertise of these college students with lived experience of homelessness, coupled with the work of homeless youth advocates, has led to new laws that improve access to housing and postsecondary education. These [California state] laws include creating an on-campus housing priority for homeless students, requiring that public universities develop a plan to house students during academic breaks (AB 1228, 2015), and enshrining a state hiring preference for homeless and formerly incarcerated youth up to age 26 for paid student and internship positions (AB 1840, 2016).

We built on the momentum of successful legislation and helped spearhead AB 801, the [California] Homeless Youth Success in Higher Education Act. Most significantly, this law requires the designation of a homeless liaison to inform students about financial aid and provide connections to on-campus and community resources. It also gives students experiencing homelessness priority when registering for classes at California's public colleges and universities (requests of University of California). Together, we believe these provisions will meaningfully help more students successfully enroll in and complete college. Personally, it's been an incredible experience to see college homeless liaisons become a reality.

Next, we wanted to better understand to what extent campus resources including mental health, child care, student programs, housing, food assistance, and transportation were offered for students experiencing homelessness on California Community College (CCC), California State University (CSU), and University of California (UC) campuses. Our findings are published in *Resources Supporting Homeless Students at California's Public Universities and Colleges* (Au & Hyatt, 2017). We plan to replicate this research in the coming years to help gauge progress and identify persistent gaps.

In the spring of 2018 we partnered with the American Civil Liberties Union of Southern California to survey California's homeless liaisons to identify the scope of their work, top student needs, and challenges in meeting those needs. To support our friends in the field working directly with students experiencing homelessness, we listened to the obstacles they face and published *Supporting California's Homeless & Low-Income College Students: A Practical Guide* (2018) in partnership with SchoolHouse Connection, providing concise overviews on the top 5 needs of homeless and low-income students at the CCCs, CSUs, and UCs as reported by college homeless liaisons: connection to housing resources, CalFresh application assistance, FAFSA completion assistance, mental health services, and access to supportive services outside of the school setting.

As a researcher, policymaker, advocate, former homeless college student, and graduate, it's important for me to remember that the work ahead of us is great, but it is possible if we're all in this together.

California also passed a law (AB 1995) that enables students who experience homelessness to access school showers. In particular, students attending institutions without an on-campus housing option may not have access to a shower. A student living in a garage or storage room, for example, would be unable to consistently use a shower. The law allows students an opportunity to use showers in the locker rooms or other places on campus. Given the social stigma of poor hygiene, this policy affords students the opportunity to shower before class—which is important for developing peer and instructor relationships that could be important for personal, academic, and professional development.

Several states have developed tuition policies. Some allow students experiencing homelessness to receive a tuition waiver under certain conditions. Other states allow unaccompanied students to receive in-state tuition. Many of these policies are expansions of supports provided for marginalized students, including those who are low-income or connected to the foster care system. See Table 3.1 for a list of policies and relevant state laws that support higher education students with housing insecurity.

CONCLUSION

Understanding the social and political context allows educational professionals the ability to have a more nuanced understanding of how and why college students experience housing insecurity. Recognizing the complexity of issues may create more empathy when interacting with students. In addition, you may find more creative solutions when exploring how other institutions have implemented and expanded federal and state policies. We encourage you to be aware of policy developments as well as engaging in advocacy for local, state, and federal policies.

Table 3.1. State Policies Related to Housing Insecurity and Higher Education

Policy Topic	State Law	Brief Description
Housing priority	California AB 1228	Public universities and community colleges must give students experiencing homelessness priority access to residence halls and year-round housing (colleges without residence halls are excluded).
	Louisiana HB 906	Public universities with housing over breaks should give students experiencing homelessness priority access. And public institutions may develop housing plans to support these students.
Enrollment priority	California AB 801	Students experiencing homelessness get priority enrollment in public universities and community colleges.
Tuition and fee waivers	California AB 801	Students experiencing homelessness are exempt from student fees at community colleges.
	Florida Statute 1009.25	Students experiencing homelessness are exempt from tuition and fees at public universities and community colleges, including the workforce education program.
	Maryland HB 482	Students who are unaccompanied and homeless under age 25 are exempt from tuition for 5 years at public universities and community colleges (excludes post-bachelor education).
In-state tuition	Colorado HB 16-1100	Individuals under age 22 who are unaccompanied and homeless can establish in-state residency without a guardian.
	Louisiana HB 906	Postsecondary institutions may offer in-state residence if the individual is under 19 years old, currently living in the state, and had been homeless within the past 2 years.
Showers	California AB 1995	Students experiencing homelessness while attending community college get access to campus showers.

EBT Restaurant Meals Program (RMP)	California AB 1894 (2018) College Student Hunger Relief Act	This law further improves access to federal anti-hunger benefits for California's low-income college students by expanding the CalFresh Restaurant Meals Program to all CSU locations regardless of whether or not their county has chosen to participate in the program for the nonstudent population. It requires on-campus cafeterias on California public colleges to participate in the CalFresh Restaurant Meals Program, which allows eligible homeless, disabled, and/or elderly (ages 60 and above) CalFresh benefit recipients to use their CalFresh benefits to purchase hot, prepared food from participating restaurants.
Food pantries, CalFresh, meal sharing, and food recovery	California SB 85 (2018) California Hunger Free Campus Initiative	The bill allocated $7.5 million to the three segments of the California public higher education: California Community Colleges, California State University, and University of California. To be designated a "hunger-free campus" and be awarded funds from the bill, a college or university would need to have a campus food pantry, offer CalFresh Application Assistance on campus, and offer campus meal sharing and food recovery programs.
Clarification of college student exemptions for CalFresh	California AB 214 (2017) California Hunger Free Act	This law further improved access to federal anti-hunger benefits for California's low-income college students.
Electronic Benefits Transfer (EBT)	California AB 1747 (2016) College Student Hunger Relief Act	This law requires universities and colleges receiving public funds to accept the Electronic Benefit Transfer (EBT) card through which low-income Californians receive CalFresh and CalWORKs benefits and to make services available to students without fee or surcharge.

Application to Your Campus

Creating and consistently implementing institutional policies frames how your students experience attending your institution. While we recommend conducting an internal evaluation to ensure your institution meets federal and state law, we also encourage you to consider developing institutional policies that expand supports in order address the specific needs of your students.

- Research the federal and state policies that directly influence your institution. Creating a resource document with concise information would be important as you start distributing the information across campus. After this information is gathered, it should be shared with leadership, staff, and faculty. Even if an individual does not work in a specific department, it is important they know students' rights. For example, a faculty member may encounter a student struggling academically due to financial and housing issues. Having information about financial aid policy may encourage the instructor to refer the student for support.
- Conduct an internal review to ensure institutional policies adhere to federal and state laws. Are there specific departments on campus that may need assistance (or encouragement) to conduct an internal audit of polices? For example, does the financial aid office need support in figuring out how to help students complete FAFSA?
- Consider the broader social context of your institution. What are the social and political issues that frame the issue on your campus and in your community? Are there partners or allies that should be included in efforts to support your students?

CHAPTER 4

Trauma-Informed and Sensitive Colleges

Basic needs insecurity undermines your students' academic engagement in multiple ways. Hunger limits energy and focus. Housing insecurity creates high levels of stress. In addition, the experiences related to lacking consistent access to food and housing may result in multiple challenges that directly and indirectly influence students' ability to persist until degree completion. In this chapter we discuss how your institution can draw from trauma-informed research to increase the retention of students experiencing housing insecurity.

Before engaging in a discussion of trauma-informed approaches, we feel it is important to distinguish between labeling students and creating an approach to serving them. We strongly discourage institutions from labeling students as "traumatized" in order to gain access to supports. There is no need to create another stigmatizing label to identify students. Rather, we advocate for institutions to carefully reflect on how they approach responding to students with financial need. Are you creating opportunities for students experiencing food and housing insecurity to thrive? Or are there unnecessary barriers that further complicate their access to the institution and success once enrolled? In what ways could you be more empathetic and compassionate in how services are designed and distributed? A trauma-informed approach is about institutional reflection, not student identification.

In the section that follows, we begin with a discussion about trauma and trauma-informed approaches. We then share a trauma-informed model that can help postsecondary institutions reflexively consider how to support students.

WHAT IS (AND IS NOT) TRAUMA

Trauma and *trauma-informed care* have become buzzwords in the field of education and social services. As with all popular concepts, the development of the concept emerged after careful research and theorizing resulted in a helpful way to think about and address issues. However, buzzwords can also get overutilized in ways that dilute and undermine their usefulness. Every disappointment should not be labeled trauma. Most college students will go through relationships that end, receive poor grades on an assignment, and miss out on a desired opportunity. Generally speaking, these are not trauma. Life involves challenges. We strongly encourage you to protect the concept of *trauma* in order to be able to employ it strategically to make meaningful change. The term has the most power to create institutional change when it is distinctly attached to experiences that create a significant impact on individuals' cognitive functioning.

Trauma-informed care emerged out of research that illustrates how individuals' brains could be significantly impacted by trauma (Craig, 2016). Educational scholars and practitioners drew from that work to create trauma-informed frameworks for K–12 institutions (Craig, 2016, 2017; Steele & Malchiodi, 2012). Although trauma-informed care has primarily been used to understand how to support students under the age of 18, colleges and universities are beginning to see the importance of understanding how trauma frames student experiences (Hallett & Crutchfield, 2017).

Susan Craig (2016) clearly explains the importance of looking at the person, and *not* the event, when considering if a situation involves trauma. Craig argues,

> Events are not traumatic in and of themselves; they become traumatic when they exceed a person's capacity to cope. In other words, trauma depends not only on the event, but also on the absent or limited resources available to help a person respond to the situation, manage, and return to a sense of calmness and control. (p. 16)

In this way trauma-informed care is not a deterministic approach that suggests all individuals who face a particular situation will have a predetermined outcome. As you probably recognize from your personal and professional experiences, students in similar situations can have dramatically different responses.

We encourage you to separate stress and discomfort from trauma. Attending college involves certain times of stress and discomfort that can be essential components of personal and academic growth. Learning to balance studying for multiple tests during finals week can teach students time management skills. Moving out of a parent's home and into a residence hall may involve learning how to get along with people from different backgrounds and enables individuals to explore how they want to structure their lives. There are many other examples that you probably can identify that involve healthy and productive forms of stress and discomfort, which are important parts of individual growth and development. Trauma-informed approaches do not involve removing these aspects of the educational experiences. Doing so would run counter to the mission of most postsecondary institutions.

You want to encourage and support your students' development as they move through the educational process.

So, when do stress and discomfort become trauma? The distinction involves exploring individuals' ability to deal with situations that are beyond their control and exceed what they can handle (Craig, 2016). The Center for Youth Wellness (2014) offers further clarification by distinguishing among three forms of stress that your students may encounter: positive, tolerable, and toxic stress. *Positive stress* allows individuals to grow and learn. Learning difficult concepts in statistics class or interviewing for an internship are generally positive forms of stress. You want to continue providing students these opportunities to grow. *Tolerable stress* involves negative situations that may be severe, but have limited duration and can be negotiated when given support. Loss of a loved one, failing a class, and illness may be tolerable forms of stress that your students experience. Carefully designed programs and resources can help students handle these forms of stress in ways that allow them to continue their educational pursuits. *Toxic stress* exceeds what is tolerable and involves "extreme, frequent, or extended activation of the body's stress response" (Johnson, Riley, Granger, & Riis, 2013, p. 320). For example, not having basic needs met is *never* positive for one's growth and development. Unlike learning time management skills during finals week, lacking access to food and housing can create significant traumas that may negatively impact a student's ability to remained engaged with school. You want to find ways to limit these situations and create supports for your students who experience toxic stress.

As mentioned above, individuals respond differently to stress. Some of your students may recover quickly from tolerable or toxic stress, while others may have long-term negative impacts that frame their feelings of safety, the ways they build relationships, their sense of self, and their view of the future (Coates & McKenzie-Mohr, 2010; Cole et al., 2005; Hopper, Bassuk, & Olivet, 2010; Perkins & Graham-Bermann, 2012). Trauma associated with toxic stress does not relate to an individual's "strength" to endure. Your students' responses to toxic stress are a rational and natural reaction to their brains attempting to protect them (Babcock & Ruize de Luzuriaga, 2016; Craig, 2016).

Trauma caused by toxic stress may be difficult to identify because it is often not visible (Cole et al., 2005). Within the higher education context, students may have limited interactions with institutional agents. Classes generally focus on a particular topic area and lecture halls involve an instructor giving information to students. An instructor could go through an entire semester without knowing that a student in the class was experiencing a traumatic event. Student affairs programming may allow for these forms of engagement, but students would need to know about and seek out these opportunities. In addition, individuals express trauma and pain in a variety of ways. While some students may reach out and be grateful for support, others will withdraw or become assertive and aggressive. All of these protective coping skills can be difficult to understand for practitioners or administrators who are unfamiliar with trauma. Staff may feel fortified when students "act appreciative" and exert harsh responses when students seem ambivalent or ungrateful when accessing services.

Neuroscientists explain how our brains are a social organ (Craig, 2016). Interactions with other people frame how an individual's brain develops. As a result, an individual who experiences trauma can also be positively influenced by interactions with people (National Child Traumatic Stress Network, 2014). Addressing issues of trauma require concerted effort and a rethinking of how the institution designs, advertises, and implements supports.

BECOMING A TRAUMA-INFORMED AND SENSITIVE COLLEGE

Educators in K–12 systems have begun to recognize how trauma influences educational experiences and outcomes for students. Recent work has explored the traumas associated with poverty and other forms of social marginalization. Scholars have developed models that help explain how trauma-sensitive schools can improve the educational outcomes for

Useful Resource: Trauma Learning Policy Initiative

The Trauma Learning Policy Initiative (TLPI) summarizes and translates research into practice. In particular, TLPI provides numerous resources related to how trauma-informed care can be utilized to positively influence educational practices and policy development. While the effort specifically focuses on preschool through high school students, TLPI can be useful for higher education professionals in several ways:

- The website has publications, videos, and blogs that provide a detailed explanation of what trauma is and how it influences education.
- The initiative has had success in developing institutional- and state-level policies. Higher education professionals can utilize TLPI efforts to create policies that similarly support college students.
- Many postsecondary institutions enroll students with children. The TLPI resources may provide useful guidance when working with a parenting student who is experiencing trauma.
- As colleges and universities collaborate with local communities and school systems, TLPI resources may allow practitioners to explore how trauma may or may not relate to those efforts.

all students, not just those who have experienced significant trauma (e.g., Craig, 2016, 2017). Postsecondary institutions and scholars have yet to fully embrace how to use these trauma-informed frameworks to more fully serve college students. We draw from our earlier work to present a trauma-informed model for colleges and universities with a focus on how to encourage the educational engagement and persistence for students experiencing homelessness and housing insecurity. This model lays the groundwork for the information shared in Chapters 5–8.

The process of reorienting a college or university to become more trauma informed may seem abstract or impossible. The current bureaucratic structures that are embedded with history and politics can feel immoveable. Often, changes are met with skepticism related to perceived limited resources or lack of political will. We understand the reality that many institutions face. As a result, we draw from previous research and theory that recognizes the importance of making strategic decisions based upon your institutional data. You can employ data-driven justifications for why a trauma-informed approach relates to your institution's mission.

Becoming a trauma-informed institution will not happen overnight. And it is not an isolated program housed in a specific department on campus. This will be a process. And it involves thoughtful decision making that utilizes institutional and community resources in ways that address your students' needs and goals. Cyekeia Lee, once a financial aid administrator and now the director of community collaboration for The Kalamazoo Promise in Michigan, shares her first experience in working with a student experiencing homelessness.

Developing Trauma-Informed Policies and Practices

Cyekeia Lee, *director of community collaboration, The Kalamazoo Promise*

I can vividly remember the first student I helped, whose life catapulted me into this work; work that I had no idea would extend beyond my office on campus, beyond my campus itself, and put me on the front lines battling student homelessness and food insecurity. Alex was a shy 19-year-old, African American man that came to my office in September desperately seeking help and resources. It was not unusual for me to see students cry in the lobby of the Financial Aid Office at the start of the semester; however, I could tell from his tears that there was much more than frustration about a delay in his aid disbursing. Alex confided that he was not only homeless, but also that he identified as LGBT. His parents had disowned him as a result, and he had no place to live and no one to turn to.

I told Alex that I could walk him through the process to complete his FAFSA, and I could make some calls to campus housing to explore an extension on his housing payment while he waited for his financial aid. I thought that would dry up the tears, but it didn't. He ended by telling me that he was HIV positive and using drugs to cope. I froze, not because of these additional revelations, but because he was so young trying to deal with these aspects of his life on his own, and still trying to earn a degree. I looked up churches that hosted AA meetings in our nearby Detroit community, handed him a list of resources, and sent him to the housing office. In that moment it dawned on me that my training as a financial aid administrator hadn't prepared me to work with homeless students. I really didn't know which resources to connect him to on my campus or in my community. I just went with the first things that came to mind. It wasn't until a year later that I found out that Alex had left campus. Unless students walked right into our offices, we wouldn't know who they are, or where to find them. Every student I helped from that moment on, I helped as if I had one more chance to help Alex.

A year later I became the director of higher education initiatives at the National Association for the Education of Homeless Children and Youth (NAEHCY), which is dedicated to removing education barriers and providing supports for homeless students from birth through college. We built statewide networks in 17 states to help homeless students transition from high school to college, identified more than 400 campuses that implemented resources to help homeless and foster students, and supported change in federal legislation to streamline the financial aid process for homeless students.

In this work I was hopeful that everyone would understand the complexities these students face and not have the need to question, demand answers, judge, and prod into these students' lives. However, I found that we still had more work to do in the field to be trauma informed and sensitive to the needs of these students. It's important to know that students deserve to go to any postsecondary education institution of their choice. It's hard for students to walk into an office, disclose the one thing that makes them feel like they don't belong, only to not be believed by the person receiving them. For a campus to truly become trauma informed, staff, faculty, and administrators have to look not only at the homeless numbers for students completing the FAFSA on their campus, state, city, and community. They have to listen to students, provide spaces for students to share their voices, and become more aware of how to remove barriers so that students will get to fulfilling their goals and dreams.

Figure 4.1 provides a visual illustration of becoming a trauma-informed and sensitive college. As becomes clear when we discuss each stage in the following chapters, trauma-informed educational institutions reframe how they think about supporting students (Craig, 2016; Hallett & Skrla, 2017; Steele & Malchiodi, 2012). In particular, colleges and universities that employ a trauma-informed approach to understanding basic needs insecurity among their students recognize the need to thoroughly evaluate

Figure 4.1. Becoming a Trauma-Informed and Sensitive College (TISC) Model

Localizing
Understanding the issue within your institutional context

Evaluating
Exploring how students experience navigating your institution

Implementing
Transforming your institution to be trauma informed

Sustaining
Creating a plan to continuously review and update your institution's policies

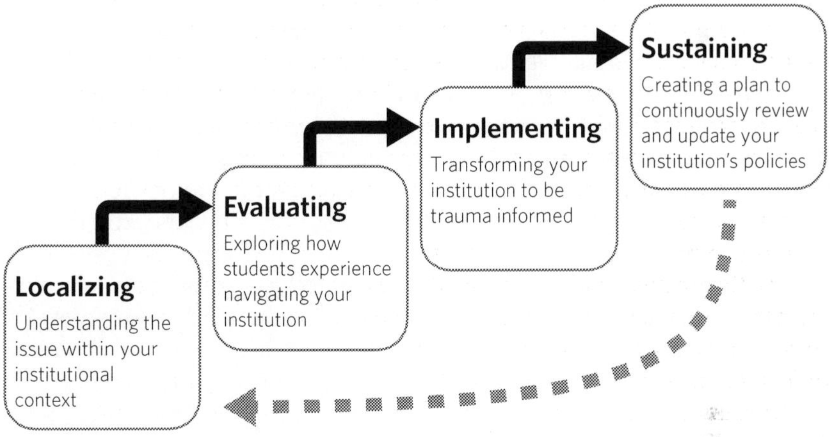

Note: Adapted from Hallett and Crutchfield (2017) and Craig (2016, 2017).

themselves in order to improve students' experiences and outcomes (Hallett & Crutchfield, 2017). The goal is to change as an institution in order to support your students.

Often, becoming more trauma informed means building bridges across possible interlocking responses to a variety of programs and services intended to respond to a variety of marginalized groups. Crutchfield and Maguire (2018) found that students of color are most likely to access services such as campus food pantries, but are also most likely to report experiencing barriers to services. This spotlights the potential for strategies that expand awareness of available on-campus resources and work toward achieving equitable outcomes. Intentional partnerships among on-campus programs where students regularly seek support (e.g., cultural centers, student clubs, wellness and recreational activity centers) are key intersections that will aid early identification of and referrals for students who are food or housing insecure.

The Trauma-Informed and Sensitive College (TISC) model is a systematic approach that you can modify to meet the needs of your college or university context. The *localizing stage* allows you to gain an initial understanding of how housing insecurity manifests on your campus. We encourage you to identify formal and informal efforts intended to support students experiencing homelessness and housing instability. During this stage, you are encouraged to identify stakeholders on campus and in the community who can assist with the remaining stages.

The *evaluation stage* focuses on gaining a deeper understanding of students' experiences with housing insecurity and successes as well as challenges in navigating your institution. At the end of the evaluation stage, you should have a clear picture of the size and scope of housing insecurity among students attending your institution. The evaluation process centers student voice in order inform decision making about how to move forward.

The *implementation stage* involves considering how to address challenges identified during the first two stages as well as how to build upon strategies that have already been successful on your campus. As with all stages, you will include representatives from across the campus to design a collaborative and integrated approach to supporting students experiencing housing insecurity.

Finally, the *sustaining stage* entails developing a plan to continue reviewing the implementation plan. In particular, you can have processes to identify issues that may emerge, including new student needs or policy shifts. Having a formal sustainability plan also ensures that housing insecurity continues to receive attention even as administration and staffing may shift in the future.

The model begins with understanding the issue of basic needs insecurity within the local context. Lacking consistent access to food and shelter can exist in varied ways for a student. As your institution gains further understanding of the issues within your local context, the next step is to evaluate how your institutional structures frame students' experiences with particular focus issues related to accessing food and housing. These first two steps are important. We discourage you from implementing programming without first evaluating the local context. The implementation process involves identifying, designing, and enacting policies and practices that will move your institution toward being more trauma informed. However, the efforts should not stop here. Sustaining efforts is an essential component of being a trauma-informed institution. Society shifts. Institutional priorities alter. Student needs change. A sustainable process should exist to ensure your institution remains focused on evolving student needs.

CONCLUSION

Students experiencing trauma associated with homelessness and housing insecurity often lack access to services and resources needed to encourage their educational retention. Institutions of higher education can create systems that support their personal and educational development. However, you first need to be aware of the issues within your institutional and community context.

We propose a Trauma-Informed and Sensitive College (TISC) Model that can assist postsecondary institutions in identifying the issue and then taking steps to reframe supports available to students. The next four chapters unpack each stage of the model in more detail. Our goal is to move from a theoretical discussion to something more practical. While there may not be a "one size fits all" approach that could be implemented on every campus, there are guiding principles that can frame how you localize supports to address the specific needs of your students.

Application to Your Campus

Consider how your institution approaches students experiencing trauma.

- In what ways do current programs and services take a holistic approach to understanding student needs?
- Are programs connected in a way that minimizes gaps in support?
- Do students need to expose their trauma by telling their stories every time they seek support or is there a coordinated process that avoids the requirement for them to justify their need?
- Are all service providers and staff aware of trauma-informed approaches, including the front office staff and student workers?
- Are there ways that faculty can learn their role in referring students to programmatic responses?
- What would it look like to do a training for your campus to become more trauma informed?

CHAPTER 5

Localizing Housing Insecurity

Trauma-Informed and Sensitive College (TISC) Model, Stage 1: Localizing

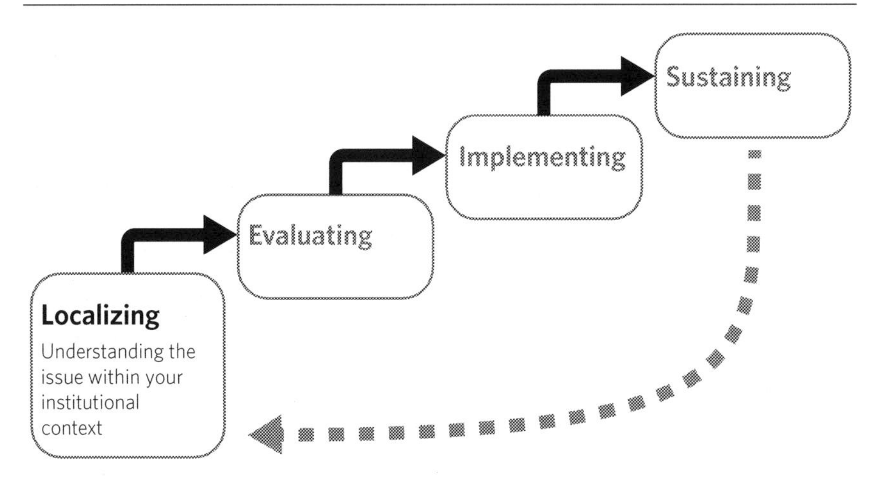

Understanding how basic needs insecurity exists on and around your campus is an important first step. Institutional leadership may have a difficult time prioritizing funding and resources for housing insecurity without evidence illustrating if and how the issue exists on your campus. In the next chapter we explain how to conduct a survey of students to get data about the size and the scope of the issue as well as conducting interviews and focus groups to collect qualitative data that can inform survey results. However, that takes time, money, and resources. In order to get those supports approved and funded, a process of localizing the issue is needed for the development of an initial plan that can be presented to institutional administration.

"The first step in implementing a trauma-informed approach in schools is to acknowledge the scope of the problem" (Craig, 2016, p. 13). In this chapter we walk you through the process of gathering information that will localize the issue of housing insecurity. Since the information you need may be located in many different places across campus, you will need a team. We begin with discussing how to gather a group of colleagues interested in addressing this issue on your campus before shifting to an explanation of what data may already exist on campus and how to present this information to your administrative leadership.

GATHERING A TEAM

Begin by building a team of individuals interested in exploring this issue within the localized context. In particular, we recommend finding individuals who are already engaged with basic needs insecurity on campus or who exhibit an interest in being involved in supporting the issue. Look for individuals who are interested in investigating the issue, even if they may not be directly working with a department or program on campus that addresses food or housing insecurity.

This is a time to bring together advocates. Later stages of the model explore how to engage with individuals who may be skeptical as well as decisionmakers who may worry about pressures placed on finite resources. While action will likely be needed at some point, this stage involves initial data gathering and sense-making to understand the issue locally. The process requires being open to the possibility that preconceived notions may be incorrect or may only partially represent the experiences of your students. You want a clear picture of what is happening on campus before proposing solutions that may or may not meet the needs of your students. Using resources to create unnecessary programming only undermines long-term efforts intended to improve educational access and retention for students experiencing homelessness and housing insecurity. The first two stages of the model are intended to reduce the likelihood of that happening.

Addressing housing insecurity involves individuals working in departments and programs across campus as well as community agencies. Even if your institution does not have an organized support program for students experiencing food or housing insecurity, there may be isolated attempts to help students. A counselor in the mental health office may have experience working with students who are forced to decide between purchasing food or shelter. A financial aid representative may have informally become the person who helps students experiencing homelessness who need additional support filing aid applications and navigating the appeals process. Admissions may have a staff member who reaches out to individuals in group homes or works with a high school that has a significant number of students experiencing homelessness. Some of the academic or student affairs advisors may have developed a relationship with students who have sought support after losing stable housing. A food pantry may have emerged on campus as a result of student, staff, and faculty initiatives. Residence hall staff may be aware of students who lack stable housing options during breaks, including the summer.

As faculty members, we appreciate that we, as a group, can be difficult to engage at times. Some faculty may be resistant to being expected to join another committee—particularly if they do not have expertise with the specific topic. However, you should explore if there are faculty members on campus who are working on related issues. A faculty member in social work or sociology may be looking at basic needs insecurity in either their research or teaching. There may be someone in education who studies how to support students from low-income backgrounds as they navigate college access and retention. An instructor in geography may have experience mapping poverty or social service supports. An economist may be researching the social benefits of higher education in reducing poverty or homelessness. A faculty member in nutrition or consumer sciences may be interested in exploring food security, health, and well-being. In addition to having content expertise related to the issues generally, they may also be doing work locally as well as being connected to individuals around the nation who work on these issues who could serve as important connections. Many faculty members engage in service to the community. You may have faculty members who work with a local food bank or homeless shelter. Be creative in exploring who on campus might be important resources and advocates. You may not include all of them during the initial stage, but they will become important as you continue to develop this initiative.

Off campus, community advocates and organizations may be working with current or prospective students who are homeless or housing insecure. A group home near campus may be encouraging or requiring residents to attend college while living in their facility. A social worker may be mentoring individuals who apply for food and housing support to also consider postsecondary training. A homeless advocacy organization may be looking for long-term solutions that extend beyond short-term shelters. Although these individuals may not have significant knowledge of the higher education process, they will be valuable resources in helping you understand how homelessness and housing insecurity exist within the local context. And they may be aware of the challenges that prospective students experience that may be preventing them from applying to college or resulting in them not attending once they get accepted.

In addition, your campus may have students who are interested in being part of the team. We would discourage sending a mass email to all students asking if they want to join a team exploring homelessness on campus. You may end up with a large number of students replying to the email who explain their need and want support. At this stage, you will not be equipped to meet their needs. This could be overwhelming for you as well as discouraging students from responding in the future when you do have resources in place. However, there may be student advocates on campus or a student group that works on issues related to homelessness, food insecurity, or poverty. During your initial connections with staff, faculty, and community members, a few students may emerge as important voices to bring into the conversation. For example, a student may be volunteering at the food bank who also utilizes the resource. Or a student affairs professional may have developed a trusting relationship with a student who might be interested in sharing their perspective.

Even if the initial conversations begin without student representatives, the long-term success of the process would be strengthened by having students involved in conversations at all stages. They provide additional context that would be difficult to identify without their voices being at the table. Given the many different life and academic issues they are balancing, include them strategically in conversations while also limiting the amount of work you ask them to do. Jessica Medina, a longtime innovator for services addressing basic needs, shared her experiences with developing a team on the campus of Fresno State University.

My Experiences as a Leader, Advocate, and Practitioner

Jessica Medina, *coordinator, Food Security Project, Fresno State University*

When starting a new program on campus, begin with a great idea to support a need. . . . In our case, it started with a student who just wanted a sandwich. My colleague received a phone call one day from the Dean's Office that there was a student looking for a sandwich. The student remembered coming to orientation and there being boxed lunches with sandwiches, chips, and a drink, so she thought she would ask around to see if there were any. We invited the student into our office and shared a box of granola bars that I had in my desk. The student shared with us that her apartment had burned down days before the first day of the semester, she only had a few items of clothing in her backpack, today was her first day of classes at Fresno State as a transfer student . . . and she was hungry and just wanted a sandwich!

Prior to our basic needs programming on campus, students like this one would often fall through the cracks and not know where to turn for help. As we began to build programs on our campus, we listened to the students to find out what their needs were. Not all students come in asking for help. Not all students want to jump into emergency housing or want someone to find money for them. Some students just want someone to talk to, someone they can trust, and someone that is there to support them when they need it. Some students are just looking for a *sandwich* . . . so we listen and get them a sandwich!

Programming started on our campus because our administrators believed in supporting students' basic needs. When you have a campus that provides support from the top down, it certainly makes getting things done a lot easier. We started our food pantry in just a few weeks. The location wasn't ideal, but in the first month open we served 198 students. Today, we serve more than 6,500 visitors each month in the academic school year.

Serving our students' basic needs is a collaborative effort. Our program has continued to be successful because of the tremendous collaboration that takes place on our campus. Development is extremely important to friend-raising, fundraising, and sustainability. By collaborating with our development and advancement departments, we are able to raise funds to grow our programs and continue to meet students' needs. Collaboration also means working with administrators on your campus. Our president, first lady, and all of the administrators on our campus believe in what we are doing and share the story of our program with everyone they encounter. By doing this, you create champions and advocates. It is also important to teach others on campus about your programs and how to best support students with basic needs. Faculty work with our students every single day. If they don't know what our programs offer and how they can support students' needs, our students probably won't know about them either.

The most important thing you can do when creating programs for students is to listen to what they need and create programs that provide these services. We can create programs because they sound like a good idea, but if students won't use them because of the way we created them, it isn't going to be successful. Continue to include students in conversations as your programs evolve. Their voices and stories are so important, and only they know what they need the most . . . but let them share their stories; don't do it for them!

If I could put it all into a few words of wisdom, these are the most important ones I would share:

- Express gratitude when students trust in you and share their stories. It isn't easy to share information with just anyone.
- Don't assume students want resources. Ask them!
- If they ask for help, work with the students to develop a plan that works best for *them* . . . they are the experts in their life.
- Collaboration is extremely important to the success of your programs. Collaborate with everyone who will participate!

Reaching out to staff, faculty, community members, and students with knowledge and experience will provide an initial understanding of what is happening. More than likely, there may already be some isolated initial efforts to support your students. There may also be some data gathered to begin understanding how students experience the issue on campus. The food pantry may be keeping a record of how many students utilize the service as well as what they need and when they visit. Financial aid will have had to verify students who identified themselves as homeless on the FAFSA, which means they have some information about student experiences and aid policies related to housing insecurity. The housing office or residence hall directors may have information about students requesting assistance. Community advocates may have a sense of barriers that prospective students experience that limit their ability to apply and transition to campus. Gathering all of these individuals together will enable people to share ideas as well as to gain preliminary information that may be helpful in writing a report for administration to encourage funding for the evaluation stage. This preliminary analysis of the campus need and context will also be useful as you transition to the evaluation stage.

You may find that this initial meeting generates a list of problems and solutions. For example, a community member may not realize that students can appeal financial aid decisions when they experience homelessness; at the meeting they can get the contact information of the financial aid counselor who works on that issue. A residence hall director may not be aware that students can utilize the community food bank during breaks when food service closes; they can get information from the community member to share with students prior to breaks. While these preliminary problem-solving strategies are important, they are just a starting point.

You may want to start with a small, eager team and then add people along the way who may be interested or have a specific expertise. Another way to approach this issue is to gather a larger group for a brainstorming session and then divide into subcommittees that can work on specific aspects of the issue in order to report back to the larger group at a predetermined time. The exact method of gathering a team together will depend upon how much work has already been done on your campus as well as upon the political and structural context of your institution. Given the variety of job duties you and your colleagues may have, it may seem difficult to conceive of a group of willing participants to join yet another committee. However, Caroline—like many of the staff, faculty, and administrators that we have worked with—discusses being surprised that so many people want to be a part of this kind of support for students. Most professionals, staff, and faculty working on college campuses have a vested personal and/or professional interest in student success. Framing this issue as important to the overall mission of the institution as well as the individual interests of your colleagues will generally yield a number of people willing to participate in the process.

Caroline's Experience Developing On-Campus Programming

Caroline, a student affairs professional at a 4-year university, explained that one of the most significant factors contributing to the success of her campus program in responding to basic needs insecurity was the campus stakeholder commitment to its development. None of the volunteers on her committee had job changes, compensation time, or raises in pay for their extensive participation. She said, "When we were creating the program, we just wanted to help students if they were in an emergency or dire straits, just get them the resources. So people just gave up their time to do it." Even though committing to the development and implementation of the program sometimes meant working beyond their regular schedules, committee members found ways to reprioritize tasks to meet the need, all while still accomplishing their traditional roles.

LEARNING ABOUT THE ISSUE

Institutions have varying levels of knowledge about how homelessness and housing insecurity affect their students or the individuals living in the surrounding community. After gathering a group together, the next step would be to spend some time learning about the complexity of housing insecurity for college students in general. The first four chapters of this book provide a good place to begin. In particular, the group may need to spend time exploring the definitional continuum in Chapter 2. Moving past common notions of homelessness will be an important step in understanding the student experiences on and around campus. Starting with a broad understanding of the issue first will enable your team to have a better sense of where to look for data.

Explore regional and national conferences focused on food and housing insecurity. For example, the National Association for the Education of Homeless Children and Youth (NAEHCY) annually draws together educators who are addressing the needs of students from kindergarten to college. Temple University also brings together researchers and practitioners from around the nation for a Real College Conference every fall. In addition to providing updated information about research, attendees at this conference share promising practices and engage in conversations about policy reform efforts. Some state university systems host conferences that provide more regionally focused information. You may also want to connect with the local school district and county office of education to see what trainings they have available. Because there are more federal and state regulations related to homelessness among K–12 students than higher education, the school districts tend to be further ahead in terms of gathering data and developing resources. Although more focused on preschool through high school, these trainings will provide valuable information about housing insecurity locally and often have sessions focused on college access. This could be a good way to strengthen connections between the local school systems and your institution.

Another way to gather information would be to reach out to researchers, practitioners, and policymakers who work on this issue. Most individuals focused on basic needs insecurity genuinely want to see progress made in supporting students and improving educational outcomes. As a result, you would probably be able to find someone who would be willing to answer questions via email, phone, or video conference. You may consider hosting a summit for institutions in your area, which could include sessions led by individuals who have expertise in the area, or bringing in a guest speaker.

We also encourage you to reach out to institutions with a similar structure as your institution (e.g., community colleges, state schools, and private universities). Although the general issue of housing insecurity may be similar across institutional type, there are also important differences. A community college may have different challenges and opportunities than a private institution. Similarly, a university that is part of a large state system will have differing resources and flexibility than a small independent college. Schools with on-campus housing options may be able to create supports that differ from an institution without residence halls. Connecting with a similarly structured institution can allow for you to learn from their successes and challenges. It may also allow you to build more seamless transitions for students as they transfer between institutions. In particular, we recommend reaching out to an institution that is already working on this issue and could provide guidance as you start thinking about how to address this issue locally.

Useful Resource: National Association for the Education of Homeless Children and Youth (NAEHCY)

Established in 1989, the National Association for the Education of Homeless Children and Youth (NAEHCY) is a national membership association focused on addressing educational issues faced by children and youth experiencing homelessness. Members work in public schools, state departments of education, early childhood programs, institutions of higher education, and community organizations to support the identification, enrollment, attendance, and success of homeless children and youth. NAEHCY offers professional development, resources, and training support for anyone and everyone interested in supporting the academic success of children and youth challenged by homelessness, through trainings and the creation of a "Tool Kit" for colleges and universities.

The NAEHCY Single Point-of-Contact SPOC Model Tool Kit is a product created by joint effort along with the knowledge and experience gained from working with college students who are homeless. The design and creation of the SPOC Tool Kit is a result of responding to the needs of higher education campus administrators, public school homeless liaisons, practitioners, and homeless students. Visit the NAEHCY website at naehcy.org/higher-education/ for more information.

Identifying Supports for Elizabeth

Elizabeth never thought she would become homeless because she perceived that experience through the lens of a stereotype about what homelessness "looked like." Elizabeth spent 4 months homeless. "I stayed on friends' couches, ya know, a couple nights in my car. Thankfully it was warm enough to where I'm not freezing to death in the car . . . [at times] my friends were willing enough to let me stay on their couches, which I am very appreciative of. What really got to me though, one morning when I stayed at a certain friend's house and her roommate was kind of getting annoyed I was there, and I didn't want to overstay my welcome . . . and I had left that day before showering, and so it really hit me like I didn't have a place to shower . . . something I would never want to wish upon anybody to go through."

Her ability to do something as basic as taking a shower was challenged in ways she had never anticipated. Elizabeth's grades slipped. When her English professor asked what was wrong, Elizabeth disclosed her experience.

CONDUCTING A SELF-STUDY

In Chapter 6 we discuss the process of gathering data to create a more comprehensive view of housing insecurity for students at your institution. However, that process involves time, money, and resources. In order to justify that initiative, you should begin with pulling together data that already exist on your campus. This includes quantifiable data as well as professional experiences and other qualitative data that help interpret numerical information. In this section, we provide some ideas of where to look, but encourage you to be creative in thinking about your specific institutional context.

For campuses that have a food pantry, the students and staff who run the center likely have some information about student needs. Often, pantries need to gather some basic information from those who visit the center in order to be accountable to donors or administration who provided financial support. At this stage, we discourage surveying students utilizing the pantry because they may already be experiencing shame or discomfort related to needing support. Being asked personal information may discourage them from future usage of the pantry or other campus-based supports. However, you may want to interview the staff and students working at the center. Granted, the students who visit campus food pantries often represent only a small portion of students who have food and housing insecurity. You may also want to connect with food banks and other service centers near campus that may be serving students. Although students often avoid these off-campus resources, there may be students who choose to access them (Crutchfield & Maguire, 2019).

The financial aid and admissions offices often have some level of information about food and housing insecurity on campus. For most campuses, there will not be a formal or comprehensive accounting of food and housing insecurity beyond the limited information gathered from the FAFSA application and appeals. Financial aid counselors may have informal knowledge about the process of seeking additional financial aid when students experience homelessness. Some campuses also have a person in financial aid who works with students to apply for federal food aid (e.g., food stamps). The admissions office may have a sense of student needs and concerns entering campus. In addition, they may be able to provide information about barriers that prevent students from applying or beginning classes once accepted.

Student affairs and housing departments often establish close relationships with students. The LGBTQ+, women's, and cultural centers often have a sense of the intersectional challenges associated with basic needs insecurity. Similarly, multicultural centers and programs focused on students who are minoritized may have some information about how their students experience the issue. As noted before, homelessness and housing insecurity often intersect with other social issues. Including an intersectional discussion will be essential to more fully understand the issues on campus.

The counseling, psychological services, and health offices on campus likely have some knowledge of student issues on campus. While these centers will not be able to give you identifiable information about students, they may be able to share their experiences working with students on campus. Professionals from these offices could also provide perspective about the impacts that basic needs insecurity has on individual development, psychological wellness, and educational engagement.

Community organizations near campus may have useful information to share about student experiences with food and housing insecurity. A religious institution or food bank may be supporting your students. The local Women, Infants, and Children (WIC), Temporary Assistance for Needy Families (TANF), or other social services agencies may be working with students to apply for federal and state aid. Programs supporting individuals exiting foster care often have knowledge about how these students experience food or housing insecurity. Services for students who are undocumented will have similar relationships with students that could yield important information. Explore the community context to see if there are services that your students may be accessing when they experience food and housing insecurity. Connect with these community members to get their perspective concerning why and how basic needs insecurity exists among students at your campus.

While this process may seem time intensive, there are ways to minimize the labor. To begin, a quick email could be sent to individuals on campus to see if they have information that could be shared. This strategy could also work with community agencies, but our experience suggests that a follow-up phone call will likely be needed. If you have gathered together a preliminary team, this task could be divided among group members. You could also invite people to a fact-finding meeting. Spending an hour together brainstorming how students on and near campus experience food and housing insecurity will generally lead to other contacts. In order to increase participation, you may want to have a phone or video option for community members. Stephen Fleischer, executive director of University-Student Union at CSULA, provides advice on linking with partners you may not initially think might be champions in the work.

Unlikely Partnerships

Stephen Fleischer, *EdD, executive director, University-Student Union, California State University, Los Angeles (CSULA)*

In 2015 I transferred roles from director of student housing to the executive director of the University-Student Union at Cal State LA. The university president and the vice president of student life tasked me to co-chair a campus basic needs taskforce with the dean of students and to open a student food pantry. I was on the advisory board for the California State University (CSU) study assessing student food and housing insecurity, and I am a former manager in a homeless services nonprofit agency. The challenge mirrored my passions for student success and support for basic needs. First the task felt daunting; I envisioned the dean and me doing all the work. When I remembered we are part of a great community, things started to move.

The dean and I created a short list of folks to join the taskforce who we thought might be interested in helping. That was an understatement. When the taskforce started to brainstorm, the list of potential interventions and partners grew and grew. The partners supporting the movement on my campus is too extensive to list. We found many partners whose contributions were unexpected and became critical to our success.

University Auxiliary Services (UAS), the campus auxiliary that manages enterprise operations and grants, has partnered with us in several ways. In 2016 we were among 10 CSU campuses who joined the Chico State Center for Healthy Communities in a grant submission to create campus SNAP outreach sites. When we were pulling together the grant, with the usual tight timeline, a UAS staff member assisted translating our thoughts into grant-speak. As an active partner in our taskforce, UAS was able to share its seller's permit with the student food pantry to be permitted by the Los Angeles County Public Health Department (LAPHD).

As word about the basic needs taskforce spread around campus, a number of faculty stepped forward to provide their expertise and support. A faculty member of the school of Kinesiology and Nutritional Sciences volunteered to supervise student interns in the food pantry and the SNAP outreach site. This direct connection with community engagement is a value of our institution. A professor of marketing and international business provides her expertise in the application of social marketing. Her techniques, unknown to us before, are helping us connect our students in need with the services provided on campus. Lastly, an assistant professor of social work is sharing her asset-building and financial-literacy programs, which not only helps students in real time, but provides necessary skills for their post-graduation future.

I wanted our food pantry to be compliant with health code. At first, I was apprehensive to call the Los Angeles County Public Health Department (LADHP), but they immediately understood the connection with food security and public health for students and were very willing to partner with us. There wasn't a clear classification for a campus food pantry, but we worked together and determined how to proceed with a permitted, safe, and healthy program. Periodic inspections of our pantry have resulted in minor modifications and great advice to ensure a healthy intervention for our students. The connection with LADHP is also crucial in our understanding of the necessary steps for future expansion to include fresh produce and live cooking demonstrations.

An expanded professional staff housed in the dean of students' office of the Division of Student Life has evolved from the initial call to arms. The taskforce, dean of students' staff, and colleagues from the university and the wider community have joined to share their talents, resources, and time to support our students. Our institutions are often a labyrinth of possibilities; if you are willing to engage all corners of your community, you may be pleased, as were we, with the response in support of our students.

You can also explore ways your campus supports students who may be experiencing other forms of trauma to get a sense of what has worked and places that collaboration may be possible. The campus may have a program for former foster youth or services for undocumented students. Or there may be programming for underserved students that focus on issues of race/ethnicity, LGBTQ+ identity, and gender/sex. How does your campus approach these and other issues? Are there programs that could be easily expanded or replicated? What lessons have been learned through both success and failure?

Gathering all of this information together allows you to begin painting a picture of how students experience basic needs insecurity on campus. In addition, you can start to see where there are obvious and significant holes in your knowledge or resistance to support for your work. You can begin to see where services on and around campus exist as well as where there may be clear gaps. Kojin Tranberg, a leader at the University of Alaska Anchorage, provides reflections from the growing response to students on his campus.

Developing Student-Centered Supports

Kojin Tranberg, *Student Life & Leadership Department, commuter student programs coordinator, University of Alaska Anchorage*

I manage a student-run kitchen called the Daily Den. It serves snacks to students twice a day, four days a week. This kitchen affords students who run it the chance to learn basic food prep and sanitation skills; meals are only limited by the equipment on hand and their imagination. It's been an incredible outlet for them to explore topics including nutrition and diversity, and become leaders in addressing hunger on campus.

My calling in this work started when one student employee came into my office and confided in me that she had been stealing food from our kitchen. She was a stellar student—a real student leader involved in student clubs, an employee of the Daily Den, and had a strong GPA. I took the opportunity to ask what compelled her to take food from the kitchen. She explained that the Daily Den regularly had food leftovers. Who would notice if she took some home? We had more conversations in the coming months, and I learned that she had also experienced homelessness while attending school.

The Daily Den has been an incredible space on campus. It has provided a refuge for students when they need a warm place to study, a place to gather for community, and food to eat. We often have students that are on campus from 7AM until 11PM. The Daily Den is a place for students as they try and figure out where to sleep on any given night. Recently, the Daily Den has hosted community brunches. With the support of our dean of students' office and Student Health & Counseling Center, we've begun providing a private opportunity for students experiencing hunger and homelessness to connect with one another and the institution. These community brunches have been an incredible opportunity for students to know they aren't alone. We serve breakfast, enjoy one another's company, and allow space for students to share what they're going through in their struggle to find a longer-term solution to food and housing challenges.

The Daily Den serves a couple hundred meals a day, and every day I'm reminded of how it's meeting a foundational need for our students. Recently, I've had the pleasure of chairing an advocacy group on campus called the Hunger & Homelessness Support Network (HHSN). This group is made up of staff, faculty, and students, all committed to better understanding the impacts food and housing insecurity have on student success. We developed a mission statement to capture the best of what we were already offering on campus and give us a blueprint for how we could continue to better deliver on the food and housing needs of our students. Having a clearly defined mission and name made it possible for our members to identify how they might engage with our group and laid the groundwork to measure the success of our efforts. We've begun to advocate for a permanent food pantry on campus, sustainable long-term emergency housing, emergency grants, and other systemic solutions to address basic needs insecurity.

I've learned over the past year that reporting your efforts and communicating progress is an essential practice to garnering long-term support for any project. There can be concerns on campus about the role an institution should play in the social welfare of its students. I've learned that creating the appropriate channels to communicate with folks quells confusion, communicates our progress, and builds momentum with current and future collaborators. Those who once believed the institution doesn't have a role in ensuring the holistic well-being of students have benefitted from hearing stories of our students. For every skeptic on campus, there is a student, staff, or faculty member that knows a student facing basic needs insecurity. Creating opportunities on campus for folks to engage in webinar discussions, documentary screenings, and other events have connected folks to be more proactive in supporting students.

As my institution works to honor its commitment to college completion, I'm confident that our campus community is coalescing toward understanding that when basic needs aren't met, student success can't happen.

CONVINCING ADMINISTRATION TO MOVE TO EVALUATION STAGE

In order to move to the evaluation stage, you will probably need some level of support from institutional leadership. The information gathered from the preliminary analysis discussed above can be synthesized in a short report that explains initial insights as well as anchoring the summary within previous research. Often, the informal data gathered will demonstrate a need on campus; however, the fragmented nature makes it difficult to estimate the size and scope of the issue. A more comprehensive approach will be needed, which is discussed in the next chapter.

In order to convince campus leaders to move resources toward addressing this issue, you should consider how housing insecurity relates to the institutional mission. While most postsecondary institutions have mission statements focused on serving students and the community, the particulars of the mission also matter. How does housing insecurity specifically fit within the mission and strategic planning of your institution? In addition, the president or other leaders on campus may have more nuanced goals. Consider the formal and informal priorities of your institutional leaders and board of trustees. How can you link basic needs insecurity to this agenda? Often, the justification relates to the need to increase student retention as well as address issues of equity and justice.

CONCLUSION

Localizing the issue involves understanding how the general issues of food and housing insecurity exist on and around your campus. You may be on a campus where most people are unaware that these issues exist and may believe that college students do not experience housing insecurity or should not attend college until their homelessness has been addressed. Often, students can present themselves in ways that hide the financial struggles they are facing. Preliminary data gathered during this initial stage may be helpful in building political will to investigate the issue further.

The process of contextualizing housing insecurity locally will also help you in the evaluation stage. Each institution will have a differing campus and community context. The process of understanding how food and housing insecurity exist within (and, maybe, because of) the context will be useful in figuring out how to conduct an evaluation.

We also recognize that getting the momentum started can feel daunting. Faculty, staff, and administrators have a lot of work to do. Adding what may seem like another task may seem impossible. However, our experience suggests that sending a few emails and beginning with a preliminary meeting will generally lead to a cohort of like-minded individuals willing to collaborate on addressing these issues. In addition, the initial group often believes that understanding these student needs and creating supports may make their jobs easier in the long run. For example, efforts to improve student retention will generally be easier to accomplish when students have adequate access to food and shelter. We encourage you to start the process and not get overwhelmed. The process unfolds step by step.

Application to Your Campus

Shifting institutional practices involves collaboration. We strongly encourage gathering a team of individuals within varied personal and professional experiences. The team should identify someone who will lead the effort. Ideally, institutional leadership will give this person time dedicated to making sure the committee keeps moving forward and produces recommendations for the institution.

Here are some individuals you should consider inviting to be part of the team (listed in no particular order):

- Institutional research office
- Student affairs
- Financial aid
- Housing office
- Admissions

- Faculty
- Students
- Community organizations

If possible, we recommend collaborating with the institution's president or provost in order to give the team some decision-making power. However, we recognize that leadership may not initially prioritize these efforts. Conducting an initial analysis to localize the issue may be needed to persuade your leaders that basic needs insecurity should be an institutional priority.

Similarly, the initial team may not have all the members listed above. A smaller group may need to begin the conversation. As the effort gathers momentum, others can be invited to share their expertise and learn from the early efforts.

CHAPTER 6

Evaluating Housing Insecurity on Your Campus

Trauma-Informed and Sensitive College (TISC) Model, Stage 2: Evaluating

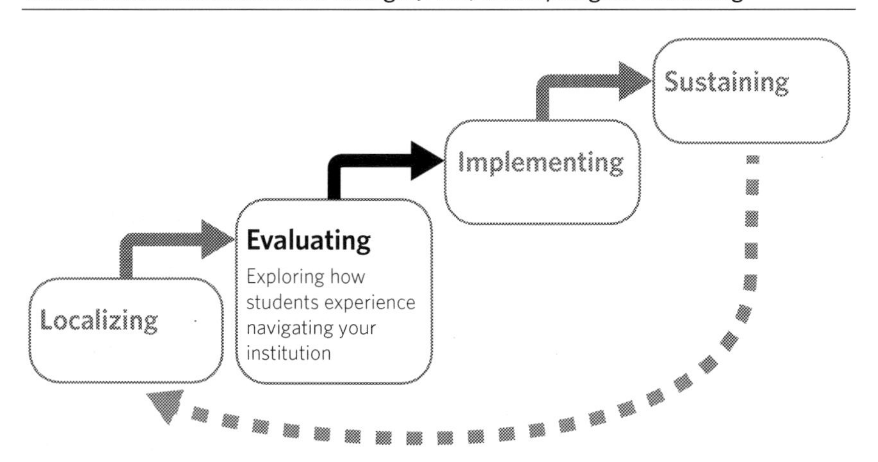

Critical to learning about the scope and prevalence of homelessness and housing insecurity on your campus is conducting a comprehensive evaluation of your students' experiences. The information you gathered during the localizing stage provided the rationale for whether or not further evaluation was needed. Hopefully, your initial research also helped you identify a network of institutional champions to support the evaluation phase. While the localizing stage helped build momentum, the evaluation findings give you detailed information about how your students experience housing security. These data are often necessary to guide your leadership in developing a comprehensive and strategic plan, which occurs in the implementation stage.

In this chapter we provide recommendations about tools for gathering data, research design considerations, and lessons learned from our experiences. We also describe approaches for using your findings to forge ahead in your work to ameliorate college student housing instability, homelessness, and basic needs insecurity. This chapter is useful for institutions in the initial stages of learning about the size and scope of these issues on their campuses.

WHERE TO BEGIN

The localizing stage gave you a sense of what data are available for your campus. Some campuses may have little information about homelessness and housing insecurity, while others may have a significant amount available. After spending time with the data, we encourage you to figure out where the gaps exist. The following are some common questions we have seen emerge:

- How many students on your campus experience basic needs insecurity?
- What kinds of food, housing, and financial insecurity exist on your campus?
- How are you currently serving students who experience these issues? For example, does your campus provide campus housing over breaks, short-term or emergency housing, family housing, assistance securing off-campus housing, support with housing deposits, or legal resources? Where are there gaps in services?
- What are potential supports students need and will utilize? Where are the opportunities to expand or reframe current services—for example, showers, laundry rooms, and lockers for students who do not live on campus?
- Are students using available services? What encourages them to do so? Why might students not use the services that are available?
- Does your campus offer trainings for how staff, faculty, and administrators work with students who experience homelessness and/or housing insecurity?
- Are there on- or off-campus programs and organizations that directly or indirectly support students' basic needs? Are there partnerships or collaborations already in place?

We encourage you to spend time with your team to identify questions before forging ahead with gathering more data. Often, institutions need specific information about the number of students attending the campus who experience housing insecurity. The preliminary information gathered during the localizing stage may demonstrate a need, but more detailed and systematic data will be needed to accurately gauge the size and complexity of the issues on your campus. In particular, students not connected with institutional agents are not represented in the informal data collection. Collecting representative data about the size of the issue can be used to motivate stakeholders to address the housing insecurity as well as enabling administrative leaders to determine where it fits within institutional priorities. You may also want data about the types of housing insecurity that your students experience. The needs of students living in a shelter differ from those who are doubled up. Gathering this information can create a picture of what housing insecurity looks like for students at your institution.

Maybe your institution already has demographic details about student homelessness or housing insecurity. However, you may need more information about service availability and usage. You may be curious about why some students access services and other students do not. There may be some services that get used at a higher frequency than others, but you know that student data suggest that both are needed. You may be proposing a new service and want guidance from students about what it should look like or how it should be advertised.

There are a number of questions that could be used to frame the evaluation stage. Based upon resources available, you may need to prioritize the most important and relevant questions for your campus. You should work closely with your team to clearly identify the guiding questions and then select evaluation tools that will yield the most useful data. Unless you are afforded the opportunity to conduct a comprehensive analysis, we encourage you to make choices based upon priorities identified by your team.

COMPREHENSIVE EVALUATION DESIGN

What a comprehensive evaluation looks like differs depending on if and how your institution already collects data. For institutions that are at the early stages of understanding and addressing homelessness and housing insecurity, we recommend a comprehensive evaluation design that includes multiple forms of data. This is an opportunity for staff who have already engaged in preliminary evaluation to partner with research faculty or the institutional research office on a more comprehensive evaluation. You may want to reach out to faculty from social work, education, psychology, public policy, and sociology to increase the depth of understanding of the issues students and your campus community face. Faculty generally have expertise in research design and analysis. They also tend to have experience writing reports and manuscripts, which will be useful when disseminating findings and championing next steps of the work. In addition, the institutional research office should be involved in these discussions.

In order to develop a more fully informed understanding of students' unmet basic needs on your campus, we recommend that you use a mix of survey data collection to learn about the size and scope of the issues as well as using interviews and focus groups to illustrate the experiences from the viewpoints of students. Additionally, you can include institutional data you previously gathered about student demographics, financial aid use, and the cost of living that may be helpful for expanding the findings of your institution's evaluation.

A comprehensive design generally involves at least two stages beyond the initial data collection in the localizing stage. First, conduct a student survey. As we discuss below, the survey data can provide a range of information beyond size and scope of the issue. After these data are analyzed, questions often emerge about student experiences, their interactions with support, and guidance from students about how to address the issue. This second stage often includes interviews or focus groups with students, faculty, staff, and administrators. This process is a more formal and systematic process than the initial information gathered during the localizing stage. Generally, a comprehensive evaluation that addresses many data points could take 6–12 months to complete. (If the team plans to formally publish findings in research journals, the process may take longer and include approval by the institutional review board.)

We recognize that not all institutions may have the resources or political will to engage in a comprehensive evaluation design. In those cases, gathering quantitative data as a first step may yield rates of homelessness and housing insecurity that may motivate your leadership to provide additional funding to conduct interviews, focus groups, or other data collection as a follow-up. We are not advocating for a "one size fits all" approach. Based upon your institutional context, make decisions about how to proceed in a way that provides the most useful and comprehensive data possible.

Timeline and Milestones

The process of completing a comprehensive evaluation will vary depending upon the size and complexity of your institution. Generally speaking, you may plan on spending between one and three semesters to complete the process. Each stage below could take 1-3 months, depending on the resources and staff availability on your campus. We provide these general milestones to assist in the evaluation planning process:

1. Collaboration with institutional research and/or research faculty to design data collection
2. Survey data collection; review of administrative data; evaluation of existing programs
3. Report describing findings from the survey, existing program description, and administrative data; focus group and interview data collection; continued program evaluation data collection
4. Qualitative data analysis; continued program evaluation data collection
5. Report describing program evaluation findings and recommendations for next steps

USING EXISTING INSTITUTIONAL SURVEYS

Before designing an original evaluation study, find out if your office of institutional research administers other related campuswide student surveys annually or biannually. Many postsecondary institutions conduct student surveys to understand issues related to student retention, campus climate, and service use in order to make decisions about institutional priorities. These surveys are often used for accreditation purposes. Institutional research offices may provide space on existing surveys to include questions that assess homelessness and housing insecurity.

Including questions on an existing survey can have several advantages. Adding questions to an existing survey may make it easier to standardize measurement on your campus over time, which can improve your understanding of the impact programs and services have. Your colleagues in institutional research have experience administering surveys to your students, which means they have a good sense of when and how to gather data. Your students may also be accustomed to completing this survey, which could improve response rates. Including questions on an existing survey will also enable you to link findings to many different measures that are already being collected, which increases the scope of your analysis and decreases the time students would need to dedicate to completing surveys.

Another important advantage of linking homelessness and housing insecurity to a survey currently conducted by your institutional research office is that they may be willing to help with analysis. Granted, you will need to provide guidance concerning what issues you want explored within the quantitative data. However, collaborating with your institutional review colleagues to incorporate their expertise in developing outcome reports will save time and resources.

One drawback of using a current survey is that you may have limited space to include questions. As has been and will be discussed, homelessness and housing insecurity are complex concepts. Including one or two questions will not be sufficient. You will want to have a conversation with your institutional research office about how much space can be dedicated to this issue. They may be willing to give you more space, but only for 1 year or once every 5 years. Depending on your goals, that may or may not be enough.

EVALUATION TOOLS

In this section we review tools to consider using in the development of your own institutional evaluation.

Determining Size and Scope of Homelessness and Housing Security

As of the writing of this book, survey tools related to college student housing insecurity have not been fully standardized. We developed survey instruments that assess the most acute nature of student housing status and homelessness. We include some sample questions in Appendix A, which is drawn from a much larger instrument that can be accessed online (Crutchfield & Maguire, 2017). As you review the tool, you will notice we do not use the label "homeless" because, as previously mentioned, many students do not label themselves in this way. Instead we use questions to align their experiences with the definition of homelessness outlined in Chapter 2. Specifically, the tool was developed to assess the housing circumstances of students using both the definition determined by the U.S. Department of Housing and Urban Development (HUD) and the definition established by the U.S. Department of Education. Both definitions were drawn from different subsections of the McKinney–Vento Act. In addition, we invited representatives from the National Association for the Education of Homeless Children and Youth (NAEHCY), SchoolHouse Connection, and Los Angeles Homeless Services Authority (LAHSA) to consult on the development of the questions used for this tool.

Federal Definitional Approaches

U.S. Department of Housing and Urban Development (HUD):

- At a shelter
- In a camper
- In transitional housing or independent living program
- At a group home (e.g., halfway house or residential program for mental health or substance abuse)
- At a treatment center (e.g., detox or hospital)
- Outdoor location such as street, sidewalk, or alley; bus or train stop; campground or woods; park, beach, or dry riverbed; under bridge or overpass
- In a closed area/space with a roof not meant for human habitation such as abandoned building; car or truck, van, RV, or camper; encampment or tent; or unconverted garage, attic, or basement

U.S. Department of Education:

- All HUD indicators listed above
- Staying with a relative, friend, or couch surfing due to financial need or crisis
- At a hotel or motel due to financial need or crisis
- Living in a doubled-up residence as a result of financial need or crisis

The questions in the survey tool measure indicators of homelessness both in the past 30 days and also 12 months based on HUD and McKinney–Vento definitions of homelessness. We suggest asking both time periods for two reasons. First, it is important to understand whether a student experiences homelessness in the past 12 months to account for housing instability during summer, seasonal breaks, or time prior to enrolling in college. Second, knowing whether a student has experienced homelessness in the past 30 days provides an assessment of the current level of homelessness on your campus. Additionally, we suggest asking students about the number of moves made in the past 12 months as another indicator of housing security.

Food Security

Given that many students experience food insecurity in conjunction with homelessness and housing insecurity, you may want to also capture these data at the same time. To find the average rate of food security on your campus, we strongly recommend using the U.S. Adult Food Security Survey Module as it has been used widely to document college student food security (Nazmi et al., 2018). There are multiple variations of the food security module to choose from depending on your institution's needs and capacity. For more details, we point you to a guide titled *Researching Basic Needs in Higher Education* (Crutchfield & Maguire, 2017).

Campus Supports

There are also survey questions available to learn more about supports and resources students access on campus. Students can be asked about usage patterns, including why they may not be engaging in services, to learn what supports or barriers exist in accessing services from students' perspectives. There may be a variety of reasons that students may not access resources and we provide sample questions (see Appendix A). These questions should be adapted specifically to your institution. Katharine Broton, assistant professor at the University of Iowa, provides her expertise in researching these issues.

Using Survey Research

Katharine M. Broton, *assistant professor, University of Iowa*

For close to a decade, I have studied basic needs insecurity in higher education, but I never sought to do this work. As a sociologist of education, I wanted to understand the daily, lived realities of college students, and to do so, I did something that practitioners do all the time—I listened to students. My colleagues and I heard students describe how they struggled to get enough to eat and secure a safe, stable place to live. Through these conversations, we identified certain student experiences—including homelessness and housing insecurity—and we wanted to learn how widespread these challenges were and how such experiences varied across students and institutions. So it was only after speaking with students, identifying a clear research question, and confirming that there were no existing data available that we developed a survey instrument to assess the prevalence of basic needs insecurity on college campuses (Broton & Goldrick-Rab, 2018; Goldrick-Rab et al., 2015). In this snapshot, I share some of the lessons that I have learned in doing this work:

1. The ubiquitous nature of surveys in our everyday lives may give the impression that they are relatively easy, simple, and affordable to do well, but this is a misconception. A high-quality survey study requires designing a valid and reliable survey questionnaire; acquiring institutional review board and administrative permissions; drawing appropriate samples; determining a suitable mode; recruiting individuals to participate; collecting, processing, and analyzing data; interpreting results; and sharing the findings with stakeholders. Coordinating a team with the necessary content and methodological expertise and securing financial support is an essential part of the process.
2. Surveys are designed to answer certain types of research questions, including those about the prevalence and distribution of experiences, behaviors, attitudes, interests, knowledge, and demographics. Their greatest strength lies in their ability to describe a particular target population, such as all undergraduates at a college. Different types of research questions, such as how students who are homeless and housing insecure perceive institutional outreach programs, are better examined with qualitative research methods like interviews, focus groups, or ethnographic studies. Before beginning any study, it is critical to ensure a proper fit between the goals or purpose and the research approach.
3. In designing a survey questionnaire, question wording, order, and format are critical components (e.g., Bradburn, Sudman, & Wansink, 2004; Krosnick & Presser, 2010). Broad concepts, like housing insecurity and homelessness, must be defined and transformed into measures or questions that are valid and reliable. For instance, researchers often use multiple behavior-based questions to assess the prevalence of homelessness (e.g., temporarily stay in a shelter or sleep in a car) rather than a single question that asks individuals to self-identify with the stigmatizing term. Thus, I recommend using standardized measures that are widely used in the research, practice, and policy communities (Goldrick-Rab, Richardson, & Kinsely, 2017). At the same time, standardized measures may not necessarily capture the specific goals or context of your survey research project. In these cases, standardized measures should be supplemented with additional

questions that have been pretested with students and evaluated prior to implementation.

4. While a sound survey questionnaire is essential, it is only a small part of conducting a high-quality survey study. It is equally important to develop an appropriate sampling and recruitment strategy to ensure that the results are representative of the target population and not biased. This requires technical expertise so practitioners will likely want to collaborate with researchers or join an existing survey research project, such as those conducted by college institutional research offices, to study homelessness and housing insecurity.

In the first half of the 20th century, asking survey questions was considered an art form, but advancements by research methodologists and social scientists have created a science of survey research (Schaeffer & Presser, 2003). A high-quality survey study takes time, resources, and technical expertise, but it can be an incredibly powerful tool in fighting the problem of homelessness and housing insecurity in higher education. Survey research, however, must be used in coordination with other strategies—student testimonials, programmatic interventions, and policy and culture change—in order to support and serve students.

Since 2015, the Wisconsin HOPE Lab (now the Hope Center for College, Community, and Justice) conducts an annual basic needs insecurity survey in which colleges and universities can participate to learn more about student experiences on their campus. For more information, see *Real College: A Study of the Real Experiences of College Students* (Hope Center for College, Community, and Justice, 2018).

Community and Public Supports

The challenge of helping students meet their basic needs may go beyond resources students can access on campus. Off-campus services and resources are often underutilized by university students (Crutchfield & Maguire, 2019). Determining students' awareness and use of off-campus resources and services will create opportunities to collaborate with local community agencies aimed at filling service and resource gaps. We offer sample questions to help you get started in Appendix B.

OUTCOMES

Another measurement consideration is exploring impacts of homelessness or housing insecurity on student outcomes. The institutional review office will already gather data concerning academic outcomes, including grades, time to graduation, and number of units per semester. You may also want information about other outcomes. Depending upon the length of your survey and time you have available, you may forgo gathering this information and draw from previous research that links housing insecurity to negative outcomes in these areas.

Health

To measure general health, the CORE Healthy Days Measures is recommended by the U.S. Department of Health and Human Services (2000). In general, this short set of questions asks students to report on the number of days they have experienced poor physical and mental health symptoms and the number of missed days of work or school as a result. Recommendations and considerations for analysis are also included in the report.

Mental Health

The College Students Presenting Problems Scale is one option to consider when exploring the nature of students' psychological concerns in relationship to their level of housing security. Students select their level of distress on a wide range of indicators related to academic and psychosocial dimensions. The measure has been validated as a baseline measure in college student populations (Erdur-Baker, Aberson, Barrow, & Draper, 2006).

STUDENT VOICES

Interviews and focus groups can be used to bring meaning to the survey data by providing understanding of the daily experiences of students attempting to meet their basic needs as well as their awareness and access to resources. Thoughtfully organized data collection of students' experiences can explain some of the outcomes you observe in your survey. Student voice will also be a powerful component of developing final reports that call for change.

Students may be given the option to volunteer to participate in interviews and focus groups at the end of the survey. Often, this is the easiest way to recruit students who may otherwise be hidden and not connected to one of your support programs. Students can also be recruited through an email or outreach through support services.

We provide an example interview protocol for you to consider in the design of your own evaluation in Appendix C. The sample protocol includes very broad introductory questions in order to build rapport with participants. Care should be taken to make the participants comfortable. Asking about life in general, how college is going, or what a typical day is like provides a purposeful entry into the conversation. The sample protocol is designed to be guided by participants' responses rather than as rigid guides to data collection or attempts to answer all questions. Please note that the term *homeless* was deliberately not used in the protocol or recruitment materials.

These interviews and focus groups should be held in a private space. Again, no signage should articulate stigmatizing labels for participants. When we conducted our study, we offered students the opportunity to participate in either interviews or focus groups. Some students would rather be one on one with an interviewer to tell their story in private. Other students choose focus groups because they do not want to be the only person responding to questions. We have found both strategies successful. Interviews often result in in-depth exploration of a single person's experience, and focus groups allowed for community building between participants who sometimes think of ideas or experiences when listening to others.

Be aware that talking about their experiences might be an emotional experience for students. They may be speaking about these things for the first time to anyone. Know that it is appropriate for students to have a range of emotions during interviews and focus groups. Students will express themselves in a variety of ways; they may laugh, be stoic, get angry, or cry. Be patient with students and do not try to "fix" their circumstances in that moment. Listen and learn. Be prepared with on- and off-campus resources they can access if they wish. Stephanie Marie Valverde Loscko of the Orange County Department of Education provides insights on how to conduct interviews and focus groups.

Experiences with Interviews and Focus Groups

Stephanie Marie Valverde Loscko, *MSW, project assistant, violence prevention, Orange County Department of Education*

While working toward my master of social work degree at California State University, Long Beach, I had the great privilege of working as a research assistant on the CSU Basic Needs Study. One of the most poignant components of my involvement in this work was conducting interviews and focus groups with participants of the study who were facing severe and persistent housing insecurity and homelessness. The willingness of these individuals to participate in this study, and their ambitious spirit to aid change in this area of need, was beyond inspiring. To hear about the adversity these students were facing firsthand was a humbling experience, one I did not take lightly, and I will always remember it as something that transformed my perception of this issue in a way that no textbook or lecture ever could.

Strengthening programs and policies around securing basic needs for students who are experiencing housing insecurity and homelessness will inevitably increase the success rate of students in higher education across the nation. Something I found so compelling about this work was the fact that interviews and focus groups would be of great importance when it came to shaping recommendations. Too often we see numbers emphasized as the main driver of change and seldom hear about the stories behind the statistics. Without those stories, we overlook the opportunity to uplift the voices of some of the most marginalized populations among our collegiate students and will often miss the mark when creating programs that are intended to help these individuals succeed. They have lived it, are living it, or will continue to live it, and without their knowledge and expertise about what the trials of experiencing homelessness as a college student entail, the likelihood of producing programs and policies that will continue to afford gaps for students to fall through is much higher. The value that was set on the qualitative aspect of this work was something that contributed significantly to my aspirations to be part of it, something I saw as integral in its mission.

My involvement in this work has strengthened my cognizance of how studies like these can promote the creation of quality, research-informed programs that can impact policy and serve as an important intervention in ameliorating collegiate housing insecurity. I strongly believe that the social justice implications of this research will have infinite possibilities to impact campus communities nationwide and sincerely hope it inspires urgency for additional research on the issue to promote basic needs programming that will not only improve the academic success of our students, but will ultimately take us a step closer toward the equitable education practices that our students deserve.

RECRUITING PARTICIPATION

How you frame the issue and approach students to participate in your evaluation process is really important. Not only do you want to increase the likelihood of participation, but you also want to decrease the potential of harm. We recommend carefully wording the invitations, surveys, and interview questions to avoid labeling students with socially stigmatized identities. The examples we provide in the appendixes give students the ability to identify with various housing situations. To increase participation in the survey, we recommend offering a chance to win an iPad or gift card as incentives. We also suggest offering food during interviews and focus groups as well as gift cards for participating.

We advise working with your office of institutional research (IR) to develop a sampling strategy for your survey. It will likely be this office that gives you the email list you will use to administer the electronic surveys. Consider working with IR staff to develop a stratified sampling strategy to acquire adequate representation from subpopulations within your whole campus population. A simple random sample can be selected within subsamples proportionate to your student body makeup. Some student groups who are less likely to participate in surveys may be oversampled to attempt adequate representation. Having a survey sample that looks similar to your campus student body can be relied on as presenting the most representative sample, even with a low response rate. The most efficient approach will likely be by using an electronic survey distributed via email with the ability of each student to be offered an incentive.

The lives of students experiencing housing insecurity tend to be uncertain. The process of data collection should include flexibility. The survey should be open for at least a few weeks with friendly reminders from trusted sources. Students will need a few reminders to participate in the survey. Consider asking professional staff who work closely with students to send an email supporting your efforts and encouraging participation. Interviews and focus groups should be offered at multiple times of day with the opportunity to reschedule if needed. Given that some students will face a crisis that results in dropping out of classes, we encourage you to consider doing all data collection mid-semester, prior to midterms, to capture the widest range of students possible.

The invitation to participation can include a short statement about how the data gathered are intended for evaluation purposes in the hopes of identifying areas where new supports and services can be created for students. We recommend deliberately not talking about housing security to ensure that you are not adding bias to their responses. Emphasize that their voices matter. While you will want to include all important language about participating in institutional research, be sure to consider how to do so in a way that is concise and accessible and emphasizes that ideas that matter to the students. For example, confidentiality will be essential. Many of these students will be telling their stories for the first time and may worry about professional and personal relationships that could be impacted if the data are not handled carefully.

Staff, faculty members, and administrators offer keen insight based on their observations and direct work with students. Utilizing their perspectives as key informants to help expand your understanding of student homelessness and housing insecurity are critical. We suggest that you develop interview protocol for these groups to inform your understanding of existing resources and supports, systemic barriers, and their recommendations for moving forward.

WRITING THE FINAL REPORT

Choosing your audience for the report is the first step (e.g., campus staff, faculty, administration, and/or community stakeholders). Defining your goals and catering the report to that audience is key. Your report will be filled with rich details for readers who want to learn more about the details of your methods or results. However, one of the most important aspects of your report is the executive summary, which will provide a brief overview of the problem, the goals of the evaluation, your methods, results, and recommendations. Keep the executive summary short with clear, simple language to describe achievable goals.

Finding key players at your institution to review your report and provide feedback will help your report be more accessible to your target audience. Consider the political dimensions of the report. What is the institutional capacity for change on issues related to basic needs and is it possible to create a system of support that increases the institution's capacity to meet the need?

Get a sense of when and how the report can be made public. Some institutions will have strict policies about this, and we recommend following up with your communications departments about your institution's policies. You may need to create a public report that is more generalized and an internal report that helps identify opportunities for change.

Template for Writing an Executive Summary

There are several parts to an executive summary that are both useful and effective in getting your point across:

1. Introduction
   - » Briefly describe the student or institutional need.
   - » Link the problem description to current goals and mission of the institution, president, and board.
   - » Link to other studies to increase the strength of your findings.
2. Overview
   - » Briefly describe the overall goals and objectives.
   - » Describe the methods used for your research and analyzing your data.
3. Summary of Results/What Occurred
   - » What were your findings?
   - » Use bullet points here to emphasize and keep details succinct.
4. Recommendations
   - » Give clear recommendations based on your findings.
   - » Suggest next steps for the work ahead.
5. Conclusions and Appreciations
   - » Be sure to include people who have been supportive of the work, especially the students.

LESSONS LEARNED

Timing. There is no perfect time to conduct the comprehensive evaluation. Early in the fall, students may not have faced issues yet; however, waiting until spring may mean you lose students who have already "stopped out" (withdrawn temporarily) of college. We suggest just prior to midterms so that students have been fully engaged in their college experiences.

Survey guidance. Do not just add "Are you homeless?" as a single question to a survey that already exists. As noted before, students rarely identify with the term *homeless* due to social shame and a general misunderstanding of the multiple dimensions of housing insecurity. Formatting a question in this way will significantly underestimate the size and scope of the issue on your campus and could have long-term negative impacts on the ability to develop important programming for your students.

You should pilot any survey questions with a small group of students and campus stakeholders before administering it. Make sure that students understand the questions within your local context. Some of the language may need to be adjusted to ensure your students' experiences are fully captured during the data collection process.

Focus groups and interviews. Seek a space for interviews and focus groups that is easy to find. Many campuses thought that putting us out of the way gave privacy, but only succeeded in making us impossible to find. Use signage that is clear but not stigmatizing, like "Interview and Focus Group Participants." Be sure to pilot the interview and focus group protocol.

Institutional Review Board (IRB). If you plan to use the data gathered to write research-related articles, you must have IRB approval. For general institutional evaluation and reports, this is not required. Remember that going through IRB can be challenging, but ultimately the process will help you think through your study from beginning to end. Collaborating with faculty who have gone through this process may make this process easier.

Use the tools we have offered; build on existing efforts. Build on existing efforts and previous research to localize the basic needs on your campus. Collaborate with campus stakeholders, including your office of institutional research, to explore data sources your campus has and expanding existing surveys to standardize the inclusion of basic needs security questions.

Build public knowledge. Sharing evaluation results in ways that are accessible for a variety of audiences will help generate key partnerships and inspire other projects. Share findings without violating the confidentiality of students, staff, faculty, and administrators who participated in the study by documenting aggregate findings without identifying information. If individual quotes are critical, use composite identities and pseudonyms to protect participants.

Share results with your campus administrators to develop policies that move away from emergency services or crisis intervention and toward prevention and higher education affordability. This may include small meetings with key leaders or large events with presentations of information to build campus support and enthusiasm.

Leverage findings for next steps. The data analysis process and findings should drive the next steps. Avoid moving forward with programming and services that do not directly relate to the data collected. Once you have support from the administration to move forward with some or all of the recommendations, you should consider how to prepare for the implementation stage. We provide examples from the CSU Study of Student Basic Needs, but you will want to make decisions that are directly informed by your data.

CSU Study of Student Basic Needs: An Example of an Institutional Evaluation

The CSU Study of Student Basic Needs (Crutchfield & Maguire, 2018) was funded by the CSU Chancellor's Office and was a mixed-methods study (N=24,537) that explored experiences of students with homelessness and low *or* very low food security. A survey was distributed to a census sample across 23 CSU campuses with an average participation rate of 5.8% (n=24,324). The sample was largely representative of the general student body in terms of race, gender/sex, and income. Student participants volunteered and were selected for focus groups and interviews based on reported levels of homelessness and food insecurity from the survey. Interview and focus group data were collected at 11 CSU campuses with students (n=213) who identified as either or both housing and food insecure on the quantitative survey.

The CSU Study of Student Basic Needs was the most comprehensive mixed-methods study of university students' prevalence of unmet basic needs and the relationship to student success ever completed within a 4-year higher education system. This study provides the most representative sample to date. Major findings include the following:

- 41.6% of CSU students reported food insecurity; of those 20% experienced low food security and 21.6% very low food security.
- 10.9% of CSU students reported experiencing homelessness one or more times in the past 12 months.
- Students who identified as Black/African American and first generation to attend college experienced the highest rates of food insecurity (65.9%) and homelessness (18%).

- Students who reported food insecurity, homelessness, or both also experienced physical and mental health consequences that were associated with lower academic achievement and nearly double the missed days of school.

We recognized that responding to students who are basic needs insecure will require complex, long-term approaches to solution building, including the following:

- Develop affordable housing and food options for students.
- Use targeted strategies to address the student populations that reported the highest levels of food insecurity and homelessness, particularly first-generation African American college students.
- Conduct longitudinal research exploring basic needs security as predictors and protective factors for persistence and retention.
- Incorporate staff as single points of contact who are trained in trauma-informed perspective in programmatic responses to students experiencing food and housing insecurity and co-locate space for the contact and students.
- Identify and institute creative campaigns to develop a campus culture of awareness and response to support students who experience significant material hardships.
- Utilize strategies like CalFresh enrollment and food pantries as preventative measures for food insecurity.

The enormity of the level of unmet basic needs among CSU students is daunting, and yet campuses across CSU are making heroic efforts to increase support and resources for students who face material hardship to increase holistic student success. Phase 3 of the CSU study of basic needs will include a mixed-methods evaluation of student need and use of services, a reporting of the current status of available support across the 23 CSU campuses, and program evaluations of support programs at two campuses (California State University, Long Beach, and Humboldt State University).

Reframing the "homeless student" narrative to encourage more progressive thinking about the needs of students may require that you engage with diverse audiences at many different levels. Conducting evaluation research on this topic has the potential to be a catalyst for change on many levels. Beyond peer-reviewed scholarship, your campus evaluation research can be the keystone to providing student activists a framework for working together with institutional partners to benefit students' health and well-being. Leveraging academic research for practical and political action can help eliminate college student homelessness and housing insecurity, and there are many approaches to sharing results.

CONCLUSION

The evaluation stage is an important part of the process. Gathering data enables you to more fully understand how homelessness and housing insecurity exist for your students. An analysis of your campus data allows you to identify student needs, which informs the implementation stage discussed in the next chapter.

Application to Your Campus

You need to make decisions about what the evaluation process will look like on your campus. We encourage you to begin by exploring what data collection processes already exist on campus. Does your institution already conduct regular campus climate or other related surveys each school year? If so, is there a way to add questions to those current surveys in order to limit the number of requests sent to students? Are there recommended questions that do not fit your campus context? For example, you may want to remove references to residence halls if your campus does not have on-campus housing. Similarly, you can adjust the wording of some questions to reflect the service names on campus. If the food pantry is called something specific, then use the specific name in the questions.

Also, consider the audience for your final report. What data will be most important and compelling for your administrative leadership and board of trustees or useful for your task force? Given the amount of effort and resources needed for the internal analysis, you should carefully develop a plan.

How will the data collection process occur on your campus? Who will design the data collection tools? Who will analyze the data once collected? How will the final report be developed? Is there a specific deadline for the report to be generated in order to impact resources for the next year? For example, the president or board of regents may have a budget approval meeting each year.

Important consideration—sending survey or interview requests to students may yield requests for support. In addition to providing their data, students may respond to the email with requests for food or housing. We strongly encourage you to have someone assigned to review the email address and respond to students, even if the response is that services may not be available yet. You might develop a list of current resources to share as well.

CHAPTER 7

Implementing Strategies to Improve Student Experiences

Trauma-Informed and Sensitive College (TISC) Model, Stage 3: Implementing

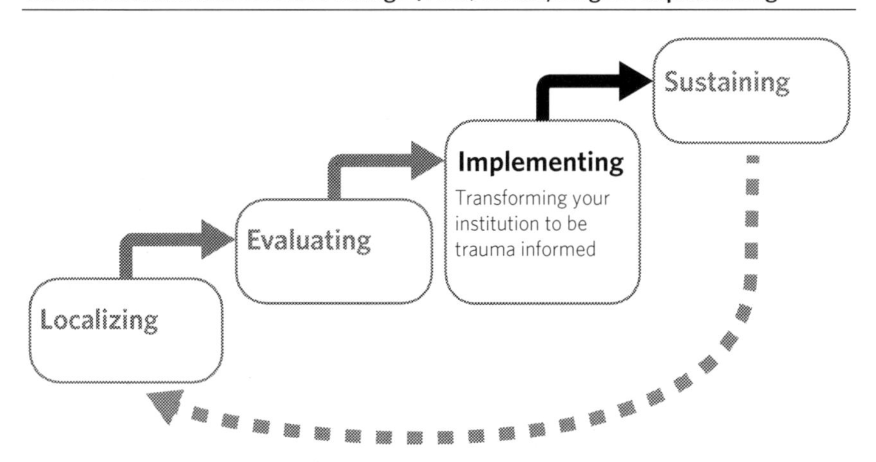

The previous two chapters explored the process of identifying if and how housing insecurity exist on your campus. Understanding the size and scope of the issue locally is an important part of the process. We encourage you to use the information gathered during the localizing and evaluating stages to develop strategies that support your students' educational engagement and retention. In this chapter we provide guiding ideas that could be used to frame your conversations. However, your campus should directly respond to the specific needs of the students you serve.

As you work through developing an implementation strategy, we encourage you to stay grounded in a commitment to a trauma-informed approach. As discussed in Chapters 3 and 4, students who experience homelessness, housing insecurity, and trauma articulate their responses in a variety of ways. Some express gratitude for support while others may show anger and frustration as they access services. Still others will avoid services until they have no other choice and be ashamed by their situation. Supports should not be designed in a way that is contingent on students' appreciation. The goals and objectives of any campus response have to consider a wide range of reactions from students. Also avoid continuously relying on students to tell their story to justify their need, as doing so can retraumatize them or leave them feeling like they have to fulfill your curiosity in order to receive support.

Explore policies, practices, and services that range from the application process through graduation and transition to life after college. Many of the ideas we share involve modest adjustments of what already exists on campus. We recommend building upon the programming on your campus that already encourages student success while also filling in the gaps identified during the evaluation stage. We recognize that not every support mentioned in this chapter would be needed on each campus. Based upon your assessment of student needs, you should prioritize how resources are directed. You may need to start with the areas of greatest need first.

In the sections that follow, we discuss some general implementation strategies. Granted, we cannot provide an exhaustive list of every possible strategy that could be employed. We encourage using your depth of knowledge about your institution along with creativity to create an implementation plan. We offer examples of new programs and services you can adapt and develop to match your campus culture. We also discuss some key barriers that may exist on your campus or in the community. However, we begin with explaining the importance of engaging students throughout the implementation process.

STUDENT INPUT AND SUPPORT

We want to emphasize the importance of including students. This includes students who have experienced homelessness and housing insecurity as well as their housed peers on campus. A collective campus approach that includes all students is essential to reducing stigma and creating a trauma-informed approach. Rather than doing something *to* the students, empower students to be part of the decision-making process. Becoming a trauma-informed and sensitive college involves shifting the entire institutional context—which includes students.

As done in the localizing phase, the implementation team should include student representatives who have personal experience with basic needs insecurity on your campus. In addition to having experience with potential barriers on campus, they may have knowledge of potential resources, and ways in which current resources are or are not accessible. You should include at least one student representative who may be aware of the multiple student groups on campus. These individuals have a different perspective of campus than faculty, staff, administrators, and community members. Individuals working for the university rarely have a full understanding of how student groups work on campus because much of that happens outside of traditional work hours. Students can serve as important ambassadors as you build relationships with groups on campus. Students at the University of California, Los Angeles (UCLA), drove pivotal initiatives that resulted in a shelter for students experiencing homelessness and a program called Swipe Out Hunger, which has now become a national initiative.

Student-Driven Initiatives

Rachel Sumekh, *founder and executive director, Swipe Out Hunger*

In 2010, I cofounded the first Swipe Out Hunger program at UCLA when I was 18 years old. At the time, the movement to end student hunger was still burgeoning. My pathway into this work was spurred by seeing the number of unused meal swipes my friends and I had left on our campus meal plans at the end of each semester while there were people in my community that did not have enough to eat.

A few friends and I decided to take action. We set up a table outside a dining hall and asked students to enter the dining hall, purchase boxes of food to go, which we would then redistribute to hungry community members. After a few days one of the dining hall managers came out, perused the scene, and slammed his hand on a box of food saying, "This program is not happening on my campus. Stop immediately." This confrontation with authority was jarring, but it strengthened our belief in the program. As we packed up, it was clear in that moment that we had to recruit dining services' support and partnership.

Our grassroots team regrouped, strategized, and built partnerships with student and faculty leaders. This was critical because, while our team thought creatively, we were unfamiliar with campus politics and how to work within the university system. These new partners brought institutional wisdom and trust to the table.

We met with the dining and housing administrators. As you might imagine, persuading stakeholders to give away thousands of dollars in retail meal credit was difficult. We were initially told there was no viable way to support the program. What's more, there was longstanding fear of setting a precedent with a meal swipe donation program. This led to initially tense conversations, but after several months of creativity and concessions on both sides, we established a program where students with extra meal swipes had the opportunity to donate them electronically at the end of the term. Funds donated from students' accounts were placed into a Swipe Out Hunger fund. Campus staff could then load the meal credits onto the accounts of food insecure students so they could access warm, nourishing dining hall meals.

We established as a nonprofit in 2012 and began coaching students on how to organize their campus communities. We have a decentralized model and only operate on campuses where local leaders are paving the way. We speak to hundreds of colleges every year, helping them identify on-campus resources and use those resources to meet the needs of students. This includes working with campus food service providers, hosting roundtables with stakeholders, and bringing SNAP application assistance on campus. We train on how to distribute meals to students and evaluate meal credit programs. The value of our work is that it is based on best practices from hundreds of practitioners. We amplify the bold work happening on campuses. We connect colleagues directly to one another. We serve as a united voice for universities committed to ending student hunger.

In 2012 President Barack Obama recognized Swipe Out Hunger as a "campus champion for change" and that helped us transition from feeling like a ragtag team of rule breakers to a legitimate and needed movement. We have added 63 universities to our network across 25 states and served 1.6 million warm, nourishing meals. I get to do this work as a woman of color and a first-generation American who grew up on public assistance. While there were and are many programs that helped students like myself get ready for college, I am honored to lead an organization that is helping colleges get ready for students like myself.

Learn more about our work at www.swipehunger.org

Student government may be willing to lead some of the initiatives. They can be a powerful voice in institutional decision making. Students in leadership roles can often harness motivation from the overall student population to take action in support of your work. In some cases, student government can be a driving force in the development of programs and services. On some campuses, student leadership roles have included development and management of pantry operations, sometimes in collaboration with student union or health staff. If you already have these on campus, carefully consider how to collaborate with students.

STUDENTS CONSIDERING AND ENROLLING IN COLLEGE

While many of your efforts may focus on students currently enrolled in your institution who experience homelessness and housing insecurity, we encourage you to think about prospective students who also experience these issues. Admissions professionals should include students experiencing housing insecurity into their recruiting strategies. We strongly discourage taking the perspective that these students should achieve stable housing before they begin their college careers. For many students, a post-secondary certificate or degree will be an important component of achieving and maintaining housing stability in the future.

Primary and secondary school districts' homeless liaisons will be important partners in the recruitment and admissions process. All public school systems are required by law to have a designated homeless liaison. These individuals have a variety of responsibilities that include informing students who experience homelessness of their options regarding higher education. Liaisons could help brainstorm ways to reach out to students and families who may be interested in higher education. In addition, liaisons are essential in verifying homeless status for financial aid purposes. A partnership between admissions, financial aid, and the local homeless liaisons can reduce the likelihood that a student experiencing housing insecurity will get denied financial aid support.

While working with homeless liaisons may be particularly useful for recruiting students in high school, that only captures a portion of potential students who may be experiencing housing insecurity. Some individuals may take a year or two away before wanting to begin college. Others may have been away from education for several years or decades and have a family. Partnering with community agencies may increase the likelihood of identifying these prospective students. In addition, community partners and social service professionals could be important connecting points when navigating the verification process for these students to qualify for financial aid protections related to homelessness.

Further, there are students who experience homelessness for the first time as they enter college or well after they begin. We have spoken with students who are pushed out of their homes when they reach adulthood as they disclose their gender or sexual orientation. Although some students have close emotional ties to their families, they become homeless because their families cannot afford to house them. Others experience extreme economic crisis *because* they are in school and unable to take on employment that covers all of their expenses. You will want to strategize how to create systems to identify students who may consider dropping out in the time between being accepted to your institution and the start of classes as well as those who experience homelessness later in their university or college path.

DEVELOPING A SINGLE POINT OF CONTACT (SPOC) MODEL ON CAMPUS

Students who need support often have a difficult time finding and accessing supports on campus. We appreciate the professional staff who have created informal services to assist students experiencing housing insecurity. While these efforts prove vital for the students who get identified, the process is not organized so that all students who have need can find the services. A centralized and coordinated effort can more easily be publicized in a way that all students can benefit. And the staff working on these efforts will have greater access to emerging policy and promising practices related to professional development.

As college and university communities increase in their awareness of housing insecurity among their students, programmatic interventions are being developed. A single point of contact (SPOC) is a person (staff, faculty, administrator) or staffed program that acts as a broker in identifying, supporting, and linking students to on- and off-campus resources and facilitates students' navigation in higher education settings (Crutchfield, 2016; Crutchfield & Maguire, 2018; Goldrick-Rab et al., 2015; Hallett, Freas, & Mo, 2018). Campuses can have complex interlocking or disconnected systems that can be difficult to negotiate while managing the stress of homelessness. Students must traverse through complicated financial aid processes and seek appropriate campus support services, while managing courses and other responsibilities (Crutchfield & Maguire, 2018, 2019; Dukes, 2013). Research and anecdotal feedback indicate that students who have a SPOC experienced feelings of campus connection, care, and success in their university communities. Additionally, SPOC staff can destigmatize students' use of on-campus supportive services. There are many examples of successful iterations of a SPOC model and resources. Shirley Fan-Chan reflects on her experiences, once as a SPOC and now as an advocate for the SPOC model.

Importance of a Single Point of Contact (SPOC)

Shirley Fan-Chan, *at-large board member/higher education committee member, National Association for the Education of Homeless Children and Youth*

When homeless college students walked into my office, probably I was the last person the they wanted to speak with. The hesitation, the humiliation, and the embarrassment were written all over their faces! In their minds, they were grown adults and asking for free handouts. Even worse, they were in college, getting a better education and sitting in classrooms enjoying lectures and the knowledge they were hungry for. But in the back of their mind: Where will I sleep or stay tonight after classes? Students told me this when they reached out to the Office of U-ACCESS, an office primarily serving homeless and foster students at the University of Massachusetts Boston. They felt like they had double identities in college: a college student by day and a homeless person by night. They felt lost and ashamed. It was that struggle that drove the program to assure none of the students felt judged or degraded.

Working with college students who experience homelessness, I learned that every aspect of the campus programming should have the college students' needs at heart. We have to listen and to understand. Their plight and struggle are different from the chronic single homeless adult or family. When higher education institutions missed the key elements of serving homeless college students, we failed them in successfully pursuing their education and ultimately breaking the cycle of poverty. Students asked us to provide services and necessities such as prepared meals on campus because they had no access to kitchen and eating areas, or pharmacy gift cards instead of toiletries donations because of their dignities and needs. It was all those small things we could provide that helped them stay on and keep going until graduation.

Navigating in higher education is daunting. Failing to submit FAFSA, health records, and emergency phone numbers could halt their academic accounts clearance. A single point of contact (SPOC) is the navigator for the homeless and foster students. The relationship between the SPOC and the student will go a long way toward assuring stability and success for homeless and foster students. A SPOC can be that person to unearth those resources and connect them in place and be ready when a student's need arises. Our role as SPOC is critical to any homeless and foster care students who have come so far in making the breakthrough in their personal journeys. They no longer would feel it was just them against the world. They have us!

Resources, including a SPOC tool kit, can be found at naehcy.org/higher-education/

Some campuses choose one person to serve as the SPOC. While this individual person can be an incredible champion of support for students, an individualized approach puts the onus of responsibility on one person and isolates or compartmentalizes support that must be campuswide to truly enable students' long-term success. Ideally, campuses develop a team of representatives from across campus who continue collaborating with the SPOC to identify and implement supports that encourage student retention. For campuses with a significant percentage of students experiencing housing insecurity, we strongly encourage creating the SPOC as a specific professional position. Adding the responsibilities of coordinating housing insecurity efforts to an already full professional role will have limited positive impact on the campus.

Student success programs are often siloed under the purview of student affairs; however, a successful SPOC model includes a cross-campus approach, including academic affairs and financial aid. Your SPOC staff must have strong linkages to staff, faculty, and administrators from a variety of departments, including representation from student life, services for students with disabilities, counseling and psychological services, equity programs for marginalized and underrepresented students, faculty from several academic arenas, financial aid, and housing and food or restaurant services. Most importantly, SPOCs can be trained and informed by students who experience homelessness to ensure that their input informs implementation of programs and services. Jeff Klaus, associate vice president for student affairs, provides an example from his work at California State University, Long Beach.

Developing a Comprehensive Approach to Meeting Student Needs

Jeff Klaus, *EdD, associate vice president for student affairs, Division of Student Affairs, California State University, Long Beach (CSULB)*

Over the past 22 years, I've worked with students whose voices and stories need to be heard. In 2014, when I was the dean of students, I noticed that more and more campus faculty and staff were referring students to me who were experiencing homelessness and food insecurity. Until then, I'd largely referred students to a case manager for Disabled Student Services (DSS) and the Counseling and Psychological Services (CAPS), supporting students on a case-by-case basis. With the increase of students, I knew that we could find a more strategic approach. We explored available resources on campus and in the community and searched campus websites across the country to find a model that would be a good fit to meet the students' needs. Many campuses had developed pantries or short-term loan opportunities, but we didn't find a model that supported students holistically with food, housing, and financial support. We realized we would need to develop something new.

Having worked at CSULB for a number of years, I had strong relationships with people across campus. I recruited a committee of dedicated campus stakeholders I knew would be interested in developing an initiative to better support CSULB students who lacked basic needs. Everyone invited accepted the invitation, eager to address these issues and support our students. There was never a mandate from above that we needed to do this, but rather the team and effort grew organically. Each department was willing to design and expedite processes to serve this effort, recognizing the need to immediately serve students. We also developed ways for the committee to stay engaged throughout the process because we wanted the community to stay invested. This cross-divisional support (Student Affairs, Academic Affairs, Advancement, Business and Finance, and Auxiliaries) built campus enthusiasm that created a program that attracted donors both internal and external to our university. Each year our program has attracted more donors, which has alleviated our initial concerns of how we would sustain our efforts.

We started the Student Emergency Intervention and Wellness Program (SEIWP) with a case manager approach and three initial core programs—the Student Emergency Grant Program, Meals Assistance Program (Feed A Need), and the Short-Term Emergency Housing Program—designed to meet the needs of the most at-risk students. The grant was created to aid students experiencing unexpected financial emergencies. The Meals Assistance Program (Feed A Need) provided students experiencing food insecurity with access to healthy meals in the campus dining halls. Emergency housing provided students who were housing insecure access to temporary on-campus housing while they secured permanent, safe living arrangements.

The on-campus housing was initially difficult because of state regulations and a shift of how we redefine what it means to support students. There are ways to make this happen, but sometimes it requires out-of-the-box thinking and/or support from top administration to ensure revenue generating operations understand the values of the institution.

We learn as we grow. We continue to add new programs and initiatives to address food and housing security. An example is our Beach Bites app that notifies students when food is available after events or activities, when traditionally this food would have gone to waste. We also added the ASI Beach Pantry, which serves thousands of students each semester, and we have a SNAP application assistance program where we create internship opportunities for students to help students. This academic year we started a new food rescue program that will allow the campus to package up leftover food from all the dining venues on campus and provide boxed, nutritious meals at the Beach Pantry. We also started Beach Steps, which provides resources to students who are transitioning from homelessness. In particular, SEIWP staff purchase items for students who are moving into new living arrangements but have no household items. SEIWP will be able to distribute items such as air mattresses, linens, towels, basic pots and pans for the kitchen. We've established partners with local agencies who provide food and housing beyond what our campus can do. These relationships are important to leverage existing on-campus support services to maximize the impact we can have on our student community.

For me, I know that this program is important because supporting students with basic needs is truly student success. If our program helps students get back on their feet, then we are doing right by the student and showing them we care. I know that a program like this can be successful at any campus because all campuses have passionate and dedicated professionals who are willing to devote their time, energy, and resources to support students.

You can find a flow chart that shows the programs of our Basic Needs Program in Appendix D and find more information about the Student Emergency Intervention and Wellness Program at web.csulb.edu/divisions/students/studentdean/emergency_grant/

LEVERAGING EXISTING SERVICES

During the localizing and evaluation stages, you likely identified formal and informal programs and services on and off campus that encourage student retention. Now that you understand what and how programs work, you can make decisions about expansion and coordination. Some of the informal efforts may need to be further developed in order to allow more student access. We encourage you to start with what appears to be working already on your campus. Building upon these efforts often requires fewer resources and the administration may be more easily persuaded since you have specific data to support the effectiveness of these efforts with your students.

Coordinate Efforts

Related to the recommendation to identify a single point of contact, you should explore ways to coordinate programs and services that already exist on campus. This would be one of the initial goals of the SPOC. During the evaluation stage, you may have found that some students were unaware of specific programs or supports. Developing a coordinated strategy increases the likelihood that students, faculty, and staff can more easily access the various forms of support. For example, the financial aid packages distributed to students could include information about the food pantry and SNAP application processes. New faculty training could involve an information session with resources concerning food and housing insecurity with a recommended statement to be placed in syllabi. Your SPOC can draw from the information gathered during the localizing and evaluation stages in order to develop a coordinated effort.

Summer Bridge Programs and First-Year Seminars

Summer bridge programs have proven to be important tools for retention for many student populations that are often at risk of "stopping out" of college. Intended to ease the transition into higher education, summer bridge programs may provide academic skill development and build social support networks, often for underrepresented and marginalized students. These programs have shown to have a positive impact on retention for students and can be essential for students who are experiencing homelessness who, much like their housed peers, may be feeling anxiety about university environments. This may be especially helpful when linking with a high school McKinney–Vento liaison who is facilitating transition from high school to college for a student who has experienced homelessness. However, students should never be made to feel individualized among their peers. Attention can be paid to their needs, but be mindful not to use the student as an example when they may not want to be identified by their homeless status.

Some schools offer a first-year seminar experience. In these cases, students may spend an entire semester in a cohort supported by faculty and staff who provide social and academic support. This model is similar to summer bridge programs; however, students can stay together for an entire semester or their first year. This can allow for the development of social groups as well as a productive learning environment. Again, care can be taken to ensure that students experiencing homelessness are fully incorporated in activities so as not to stigmatize them, but provide linkages to single points of contact who can explore their specific needs.

New Student Orientation

Colleges and universities often provide an orientation for incoming students from high school or transfer students from other postsecondary institutions. These can be opportunities for students to conceptualize their place on their campus and how to navigate it. Services of all kinds, including those directed at meeting basic needs, can be highlighted during orientations. *All students* can be given information about the supports available on your campus related to food and housing insecurity. Avoid singling out students who appear to have financial stress. Creating a targeted orientation for "homeless students" could create a sense of shame and undermine their academic or social engagement. Further, you will have a difficult time predicting which students may need the support in the future. A student from a middle-class family may enter college with a sense of financial security, but experience a financial crisis a few years later. In addition, a student with housing stability may share the information gathered with their friends who are current or prospective students.

Transition Into and Through College

While students experiencing housing insecurity have similar issues as their housed peers, there are also specific challenges that warrant further consideration. Students may significantly rely on financial aid reimbursements to cover housing, education, and food costs. Reimbursement obstacles or delays that have negative consequences for all students are exponentially more difficult for students who experience basic needs insecurity. On-campus housing deposits are often required prior to financial aid disbursements. Delay in financial aid can create an economic crisis that could lead to the student stopping out before they enroll in classes or dropping out of classes within the first month. This can be an issue in the first semester of the first year of college as students attempt to learn financial aid policies, but it can also continue to be a problem for students who are actively enrolled.

Students may not realize that their financial aid distributions can change if they gain access to employment or scholarships. They might also not realize that even though they decided not to accept subsidized loans, they can change that decision later in the semester. Further, students who were identified as homeless on their FAFSA will need to be verified again every year. If students are no longer in touch with their high school liaison or others who provided documentation to verify their status, their path to receiving financial aid can be obstructed (Crutchfield, Chambers, & Duffield, 2016). Provide outreach to students to help them understand their options.

Programs for Marginalized Students

You likely already have a range of services and social supports for students. Understanding the various offerings of your TRIO programs or programs for students with disabilities can both enhance your ability to coordinate services and build linkages with other dedicated staff. Centering outreach or implementation of services in centers that support students of color, current or former foster youth, and students who identify as LGBTQ+ can ensure these are places that are safe for students to discuss their status as housing insecure and seek assistance. Joshua Williams reflects on his leadership in support of students who have been in foster care.

Supporting Former Foster Youth

Joshua Williams, *Guardian Scholars coordinator, California State University, Dominguez Hills*

Working with foster and former foster youth students in higher education has been equally as rewarding as it has been challenging. When I began my career as a student affairs practitioner, I didn't know much about serving students who grew up in the foster care system. Since then, I have spent countless hours with students building rapport just so that they would open up to me about some of the challenges that they encountered while in pursuit of their degree. Over time, I developed a deeper understanding of the resources that I needed to seek as a professional to support them.

I found that some of the students I was working with were experiencing homelessness. I realized that, for a lot of the students who were having challenges academically, those challenges were directly tied to the fact that they didn't have a place to live. How can I expect my students to thrive academically when they aren't sure where they are going to sleep from night to night? If students are sleeping in their cars, how can they be awake the next day and listen to a lecture? Are they likely to have access to food with high nutritional value? And if they don't have a car, then what? These are questions that I've had to ask myself in order to help guide my practice in working with students experiencing homelessness.

Food and housing security are of the utmost importance as many students who have been in foster care may not have familial support and are more prone to experience homelessness than their peers. I have had to make sure that I understand the housing resources available to them because so many students become homeless during the semester. I have found it extremely helpful to form relationships not only with campus housing, but with community organizations working to provide housing for transition-age foster youth in the community.

Outreach is also extremely important. Making connections with high school and community college students who will be transitioning into my university has allowed me to link with students earlier, before they arrive on campus, which makes the transition easier for a lot of students. And because we have made a connection, students are more likely to open up sooner about their housing insecurity. In many cases, this has allowed me to help students find a solution to their housing issues before they experience homelessness and a severe blow to their academic performance. Most importantly, it has been important for me to recognize the resilience in the students I work with. And sometimes they need those reminders as well.

Community Collaborations and Partnerships

Some aspects of support require engaging with organizations and community agencies outside of your institution. For example, guaranteeing housing for students experiencing homelessness may be difficult, particularly if your campus does not have on-campus housing. Local community agencies and advocates may be working on providing affordable housing options. Your local government may have professionals who have an interest in finding workable solutions. Often, higher education institutions are not part of these conversations, but they should be. You want your students' needs and interests to be included in the development of these affordable housing options.

As you localized your understanding of the experiences of stakeholders in the area, hopefully you began or solidified relationships with community and governmental agencies. If not, now is the time to shape critical dialogue and develop strategic partnerships between higher education, public social services, nonprofit organizations, and private industries that work toward ending student homelessness. As previously mentioned, not all areas have available local resources. For those that do, it is important to deepen relationships with local food and housing programs, programs servicing foster youth, and mental and physical health services. Find out about city and state initiatives to address housing policy. Rachael Simon, who works in the office of a county supervisor, shares her thoughts on connecting to local government to support students.

Connecting with the Local Government

Rachael Simon, *MSW, homelessness policy fellow for the Office of Los Angeles County Supervisor Sheila Kuehl, The United Way of Greater Los Angeles*

I am incredibly passionate about working to solve homelessness and entered my master of social work (MSW) program at California State University, Long

Beach, in hopes of developing the clinical skill set to best support individuals and communities experiencing poverty, housing instability, and homelessness. During the program, I was provided an incredible opportunity to work as a graduate research assistant on the CSU systemwide study of students' basic needs. While I love working in direct service and understand the magnitude of such work, this research experience allowed me the opportunity to bear witness to the direct correlation between research and the creation of policies that address structural inequalities and directly influence system changes.

As a result of my engagement in the CSU research, I obtained a fellowship in local government working on programs and policies that address housing insecurity and homelessness. My office works closely with large and small organizations and service providers that serve individuals experiencing homelessness to identify opportunities for collaboration and develop policies that create systems-level changes. Local government can provide campuses, organizations, and service providers with access to valuable resources, including financial capital, that would otherwise remain underutilized or unknown. I strongly encourage practitioners to develop relationships with their local government agencies, particularly at the city and county level, and to leverage these relationships to create the most robust programs and policies needed to best serve the students you work with.

DEVELOPING NEW PROGRAMS TO ADDRESS HOUSING INSECURITY

You may have found that some of the existing services can support students who experience homelessness in ways that you had not thought of before. Still, it might be necessary to develop programs and services that specifically focus on the needs of these students. Many campuses start with food pantries to address the immediate needs. This is a good place to begin, but cannot be the end. We offer other potential program components, some of which go beyond this short-term, provisional response. Model programs can begin by addressing three key areas: food, housing, and financial distress. Social support and space for respite are also important considerations.

Case Management

We recommend having a case management model that ensures that students are met with empathy and ensures appropriate linkages to supports and services. In any case, staff should ensure that students are provided responsiveness and empathy, and are not stigmatized or made to endure unnecessary questions or inquiry. Students should be received knowing that they may have waited until they are in dire circumstances before seeking help. Staff should assess the situation for appropriate intervention and link to appropriate services. Students should not have to tell their story more than once. Embedded collaboration with offices like financial aid, housing, food services, counseling and psychological services, and other student supports are of utmost importance during the process so that when the program refers a student, they do not have to repeatedly justify their need. Financial aid administrators can be assured that students have explored their concerns and need support in adjusting their financial aid package without further constraint associated with proving their financial need again. Housing staff can know that the student has already met with a case manager, is eligible for support, and should be put in emergency housing without additional application.

Campuses that have departments of social work are often seeking appropriate placements for students. If a program has a master-level social worker who can supervise, this can be a fruitful partnership with appropriate staff and a learning opportunity for students. That said, social work students who lack basic needs should not be expected to be served by their peers. Having someone who is not a peer available for those students is necessary. Dianka Lohay, who hopes to be a SPOC herself one day, shares her experience being a student who was low-income and returned to school later as a parent.

Experiences Navigating Social Services as a Student

Dianak Lohay, *MSW, graduate of California State University, Long Beach*

I first became interested in working with food and housing insecure students while I was in community college and struggling to meet my own basic needs. My husband was deported in 2011 and I was a newly single mother of three children. I decided to quit my job, enroll in community college, and apply for government assistance in order to attend school full-time. I was deeply ashamed of being on welfare. To my surprise, I found that my community college had an entire department dedicated to students on public assistance called the CalWORKs office. The CalWORKs office provided an extremely supportive environment, which included specialized academic advising, welfare program enrollment assistance, tutoring, gas cards, food vouchers, merit-based grants, and referrals to various community resources. Most importantly, the CalWORKs department provided a community of supportive faculty and staff. I set my anchor and soon my shame turned to drive. Learning to navigate programs that were designed to help students in need became the cornerstones of my education. Fellow students who were experiencing homelessness and food insecurity would routinely approach me for help and it was along this path that a future in a helping profession took shape.

Once I transferred to a 4-year university, I no longer qualified for many welfare programs and was surprised to learn that there was no CalWORKs office. As a single parent of teenage children at the time, I was notably older than most of my classmates. There were times that I experienced both welfare stigma and ageism. My academic advisors were uninformed about mandatory welfare paperwork and I dreaded making the monthly required visit to verify my enrollment, being required to explain what I needed and why to a new advisor every time. On more than one occasion, staff assumed I was the parent of a college student, which left me feeling doubly stigmatized while explaining my welfare verification paperwork. With no alternative, I chalked the humiliation up to the cost of being a woman in her forties on welfare.

Today I am a graduate student who is no longer receiving welfare. I still access the Supplemental Nutrition Assistance Program (SNAP) and continue to visit a food pantry twice a week. As a research assistant focused on food and housing insecurity among college students, I strongly urge higher education staff, faculty, and administration to consider developing specialized departments for students in need and ensure that all staff and faculty are educated about welfare programs. On multiple occasions I have been wrongly discontinued from welfare and food programs because of my student status, and CalWORKs counselors at my community college were able to help me with my appeal. Without these programs, I would not have been able to achieve academic success. Specially trained staff that serve as liaisons between county welfare program workers and students are indispensable and I would like to see this standardized at all university campuses one day.

Additionally, staff and faculty should be trained to understand that not all college students are young single adults or free of financial burdens. I believe there is an unrealistic assumption, even among faculty, that financial concerns should take a backseat during the college experience. I would like to see universities follow the example from community colleges and design supportive programs for student parents to ensure that all students are able to achieve their educational goals.

Emergency Grants

SPOC programmatic responses can be aimed to address short- and long-term needs. Short-term responses can target nutritional, housing, and financial emergencies. Many campuses provide short-term emergency *loans* for students who experience a crisis. Students can apply for a small on-campus loan, often about $500, and may have up to 3 weeks to repay this debt. For students who have available resources, but may find themselves short on funds for an unexpected car repair or medical bill, this option is appropriate. However, for students who experience homelessness and housing insecurity, this can lead to an even larger financial crisis. Unable to repay the loan in the time allotted, students will experience deepening debt, holds on registration, housing, and other campus services.

The development of a student emergency *grant* program is often a better fit for an unexpected financial crisis. Emergency grants do not need to be repaid and, with the cooperation of the financial aid office, can be remitted to students quickly. However, in creating emergency grants, pitfalls can occur. Financial awards of any kind are often linked to students' enrollment accounts. If students have existing debts (e.g., library fees or registration costs) emergency grants meant to cover crisis events can be automatically applied to those existing debts, never finding their way to the students' presenting need. Careful negotiation with financial aid, the scholarship office, and fiscal specialists will need to occur to avoid unintended consequences.

Short-Term Emergency Housing

Short-term emergency housing that lasts 10 days to an entire semester can provide stabilization for students on campuses with dormitories while they secure permanent, safe living arrangements. Developing this service can require strategic collaborative efforts and support from high-level leadership to encourage collaboration. Some campuses may also choose to build agreements with local hotels. This can be especially important for campuses that do not have housing or for students with families or pets.

Linkages to a Continuum of Care (CoC)

In many cities, community-based organizations and governmental agencies that work to house those who are homeless are linked in a coordinated effort known as a *continuum of care*. CoCs may be provided funding by state and local governments to quickly house individuals and families while minimizing the trauma. CoCs have been developed to improve access to and support utilization of programs and services. Seek out the leader of your local CoC to understand how to coordinate entry of your students into available housing.

Be aware that many students avoid community housing opportunities and shelters. To best facilitate this process, go to housing agencies, take a tour, and meet with the people that will be orienting your students. In some cases, you may be surprised to find that available resources are not what you might think. When working with students, you can speak from direct experience about what they will see. Whenever possible, tell them the exact person who will be expecting them, and make sure that person knows to expect your student.

Safe Parking and Parking Relief

Sleeping in a car is far from ideal; however, many students find this is the only resort they have left. Many students will park on or near your campus for convenience and because they perceive it as the safest place possible. Incorporate your campus police and parking enforcement officers in this conversation of homelessness and housing insecurity. Train them on how to approach students with care and empathy and be sure they have the resources they need to refer students for campus support.

You may also develop parking strategies that allow students to sleep in their cars in a safe place. Leaders at Humboldt State University are taking measure to ensure that students are allowed to sleep in their cars overnight without being pushed off campus or risk receiving a parking citation. Leaders at the University of Alaska Anchorage are allowing students who have accumulated high fees for parking violations can repay these with service rather than funds. While many students who accumulate parking citation debt would typically face holds on registration and campus services that could lead to getting pushed out of college all together, students are given the opportunity to find alternatives that will allow them to be retained.

Eligibility Requirements

We have found that people may worry that the development of programs will encourage students who do not need services to utilize resources they do not need. While some students may hear of available services and inquire about them, we have found that students who do seek services are far and away in the most severe circumstances. To destigmatize student use of on-campus programs and services, we suggest creating a system that prioritizes student need over student eligibility for services not only to offset student reluctance in accessing services, but also to help normalize use of on-campus services (Twill, Bergdahl, & Fensler, 2016).

We recommend avoiding eligibility requirements like minimum grade point average (GPA) since circumstances related to a lack of basic needs may negatively impact a student's academic standing. Generally, current enrollment and the ability to demonstrate an urgent financial need is enough. There must be balance in maintaining students' dignity in the process while assessing for need. Be aware that proof of need, like receipts or letters of verification, can impede responsiveness in students. Given that students have likely waited until their need is dire, these requirements are counterproductive.

Finding the Right Location

Finding a program space to meet with students that ensures their comfort and confidentiality can be challenging. Whenever possible, it is important to find a dedicated space for students seeking services that is readily available to them. Hiding services in outlying areas to avoid stigma can ultimately make program options inaccessible for students who often have little time and may get frustrated easily.

When possible, having a place where students can relax and connect with one another provides important respite and community building (Crutchfield & Maguire, 2018, 2019). Students who experience homelessness and housing instability often stay on their campuses for long periods of time for reprieve and stability. These spaces can be equipped with microwaves since students often do not have a place to heat their food. Students may also find making connections with students with similar experiences helps them find new resources and build social relationships (Crutchfield, 2016). If space is available, it is an important component to supporting students. An office space that allows for private conversations is also helpful.

Creating a Webpage

Having a web presence with information about services available is important. Students may resist disclosing their circumstances to another person, but they may feel more confident in doing so if they have had the opportunity to explore available resources electronically. Creating a webpage with available resources as well as short stories normalizing students' circumstances can be a helpful tool in identifying students who need support. In addition, staff and faculty may look at the website when trying to find services while working with a student. It is important to keep this page up to date.

RESPONSES TO FOOD INSECURITY

In this book, we have primarily focused on issues related to homelessness and housing insecurity. As we mentioned, students without stable housing often experience food insecurity as well. While there are many resources available related to addressing food insecurity for college students, we provide a few ideas that could be included as part of a comprehensive approach to addressing basic needs insecurity on your campus.

Food Pantry

A common approach involves developing a food pantry on campus or collaborating with a community agency close to campus that will develop a food distribution program. Food pantries are often a first response to basic needs insecurity on college campuses and can be an important buffer mitigating food insecurity (Cady, 2014; Goldrick-Rab, Cady, & Coca, 2018). Many students welcome this type of support (Crutchfield & Maguire, 2018), and students who experience food insecurity are more likely to utilize on-campus food pantries and free food events than off-campus services.

Clare Cady, founding director of the College and University Food Bank Alliance, provides important insights about food pantries.

Creating Food Pantries on Campus

Clare L. Cady, *founding director of the College and University Food Bank Alliance*

When I took a job managing the Human Services Resource Center at Oregon State University in 2011, I was living in my car. The recession had hit the wilderness industry (where I had been working) hard, and I found myself homeless and unemployed. The role I was offered was not something I had seen in student affairs or on any campus before. They were looking for someone with higher education, counseling, and nonprofit experience. I had all three.

On my first day, I volunteered at the campus food pantry I would supervise. It was not until I was helping students pick food off of the shelves that it really hit me—my job was to serve students who were going hungry. Not one of my faculty or mentors in graduate school prepared me for this. Upon seeking resources to learn more about this student issue, I found only two published studies and no organizations to support my professional development.

I sought out others around the country who were doing this work. Nate Smith-Tyge, the food bank director at Michigan State University, and I spoke at length and decided we would work to bring people together digitally for the purpose of teaching, learning, and collegial support. With some funding for a website and additional recruitment of members, we launched the College and University Food Bank Alliance (CUFBA) in 2012. At the time we had 15 members—all of whom had pantries on their campuses to serve students. We started being approached to help get pantries started on other campuses. Over the next 6 years our membership grew to more than 700, with many members managing well-developed pantries providing food for students.

Throughout this time I have also been working on other interventions to address student food insecurity—both at Oregon State and on other campuses. I developed Supplemental Nutrition Assistance Program (SNAP) outreach and enrollment efforts, piloted food voucher programs, collaborated on ways to get lower-cost yet nutritionally valuable meal programs set up within dining centers, and worked to get SNAP dollars accepted in college convenience stores.

I have learned there is no one silver bullet that will ensure that students are financially stable while they pursue a degree or credential. Poverty is a systemic sickness in the United States, and food and housing insecurity are its symptoms. Systemic problems require systemic solutions, and these solutions must be multifaceted. Food pantries help because they feed today the students who needed food yesterday. They may not, however, feed students tomorrow—and students will still have need tomorrow. Partnering many interventions, including action and advocacy to change campus, state, and federal policy, is the only way to solve this issue. We have a lot of work to do if we want to make a difference.

For more information and resources, please visit the website of the College and University Food Bank Alliance at sites.temple.edu/cufba/

Some pantries rely largely on nonperishable items, and others include refrigerated items as well as school or hygiene supplies. Many campuses start small, but grow as sustainable locations and logistics are navigated. As a part of your localizing and evaluating processes, you likely found good places to start. As Clare mentions, food pantries are only a short-term first step in providing support for students. Many of the pantries provide food once a week or a couple of times a month. For students experiencing extreme food insecurity, these supplemental programs do not fully address their needs. Students with specific dietary restrictions may not as easily be able to benefit from these programs. In addition, pantries restrict student autonomy and choice.

We encourage campuses to consider developing food pantries as an emergency and supplemental form of support. These programs can be important points of first contact with students, which may allow you to connect them with other forms of support. However, we recommend also developing programming that may lead to long-term food security.

Supplemental Nutrition Assistance Program (SNAP) Outreach

SNAP, often colloquially referred to as food stamps, is a nutrition assistance program that supports individuals facing financial insecurity so severe that it may limit access to food. Students often encounter barriers in accessing SNAP. Federal law stipulates that students attending college or universities half-time or more are categorically ineligible for SNAP unless they meet one of several exemption criteria or work a minimum average of 20 hours per week. Adding 20 hours per week to full-time course loads intensifies the already demanding schedules of students who experience homelessness. Additionally, employment is not always easy to find, and college students usually work jobs that have unpredictable weekly schedules, which can make it difficult to prove a consistent number of hours worked each week.

Campuses can develop a program to provide application assistance, including walking students through an application, ensuring they have the necessary documentation, detailing the process utilized in your county, and facilitating linkages to county eligibility workers. Staff should review county eligibility requirements as well as exceptions for students meeting certain criteria such as students who are work-study eligible, have state grants, participate in public work programs, are enrolled in state-funded training programs to increase employability, are foster or former foster youth, or are a parent of a minor. Staff can be trained on confidentiality requirements, sensitivity, and tactics to normalize the process to reduce stigma. Also, developing these relationships with county SNAP benefit workers can ensure that your students' applications are in line with the expectations of the people who will receive them. Further, this will alert workers that they may see an increase in applications.

Food Sustainability and Recovery

Some campuses have developed programs to allow students who have paid for meal plans on campus to donate unused meals to students who can benefit from them. Meals or financial donations can be put on students' campus ID cards so that no extra coupons or other indicators are developed, avoiding stigmatizing students who utilize these resources. This often requires a coordinated effort with food services, which is typically a self-sustaining auxiliary. Coordinating this effort in partnership with auxiliary stakeholders can affirm their role in campus student success.

Campuses are also finding ways to feed students and avoid food waste. You have likely attended a meeting where refreshments were served, some of which are discarded if not eaten. Some campuses have developed phone apps that send students text notifications when meetings have concluded and there is available food for students. Other campuses have developed food rescue programs that allow the campus to package up leftover food from all the dining venues on campus and provide boxed, nutritious meals to students at centralized locations, like a campus food pantry.

Integrating Basic Needs Support

Not all students experiencing homelessness or housing insecurity also have food insecurity. Similarly, there will be students with food insecurity who have stable housing. However, a significant overlap exists. We recommend creating an integrated approach that includes housing and food insecurity programming working collaboratively. Both services should be in a centrally located space on campus. Students applying to one service should be given information about the other services. As much as possible, design services so that students do not have to retell their stories multiple times in order to get support. If different offices exist to address food and housing, the professional staff should walk the student between locations to help get the process started.

CAREER SERVICES AND LIFE AFTER GRADUATION

Many students envision graduation as both a finish line and a starting point for the rest of their lives. The dream of leaving school wiser and entering the stable-income workforce can be an exciting incentive to persist. However, the degree alone will not enable individuals to achieve residential stability after college. As many of us know, finding a job upon graduation can be difficult. For students who experience housing insecurity or homelessness, this can be devastating. If they have had access to support programs throughout their college career, they will often become ineligible for those services upon graduation or shortly thereafter. Many students have limited financial resources during their job search or during the first month of a new job, and these students are likely concerned about loan repayment requirements that will begin to kick in just months after graduation. Moving to a parent's home during this transitional time may not be an option for students.

Students may need to be connected with social service agencies to understand how their eligibility for supports will shift after college. If they go right to graduate school, they may need help developing a plan for the summer when not enrolled in school and a transition into a new program or institution. For community college students, transitions into the workplace or 4-year universities must be coordinated. These individuals benefit from career and transitional planning in advance of graduation. SPOCs can work collaboratively with career services and other offices on campus as well as community organizations to support the transition to life after completing the goal of degree or certificate completion.

POTENTIAL ROADBLOCKS

As with any new program, challenges arise during development. Though there will likely be many opportunities for on- and off-campus community collaboration, there may be some who question the existence of the problem or challenge the role of higher education to meet this need. This is an opportunity to reframe this issue as a responsibility of the campus and important to student success. Push for a perspective that focuses on student well-being.

Focus on Student Well-Being

We spoke with one university staff person who discussed how his university transitioned in how they think about students experiencing basic needs insecurity. He said, "The old philosophy was students should really—if they're in that much of a crisis situation—they should stop out of the school to 'get their life together' and then come back. But clearly what we have learned is that the support network, the system that we have here, is so much greater than what they have if we didn't have them in place. Not only can [we] financially keep them going . . . we have an infrastructure that really does support students. So the stop out really didn't make sense."

He continued, "Many staff, faculty, and administrators are realizing that counseling out students who lack basic needs, to suggest to them that they find stability and return, often means that students never return and may stay in a cycle of being on the financial edge. We are remembering that students come to higher education to create and imbed well-being and financial self-sufficiency. Asking them to find that stability before they enter college is counterintuitive."

Some students' circumstances you may find more challenging to address. A few examples include students experiencing chronic homelessness, crises during the middle of an academic break, or severe, persistent mental health issues. These complex situations often require more specialized, long-term services than most on-campus programs can provide. Collaboration between on- and off-campus services will be essential.

CONCLUSION

There are many ways to measure success. Although more difficult to quantify, commitment to students is important—particularly when that includes compassion, empathy, creativity, and activism. These characteristics will be important as you develop coordinated and comprehensive support structures. Further, advocacy at local, state, and federal levels is needed to address larger issues of poverty, affordable housing, and support for higher education to develop long-term support or mitigate or eliminate larger social problems.

We provided a long menu of options for programmatic responses to students. The implementation process can be the most exciting stage, but it can also be overwhelming. After gathering information about student experiences on campus, you can begin developing a coordinated effort to address their needs that fits your campus. Focus on what is available and expand based on the resources you have and can develop.

Application to Your Campus

Start with the dreaming stage before worrying about constraints. Based upon your analysis of the evaluation data and exploring the current campus context, what would the "ideal" program look like that would meet all of your students' needs? How would it be positioned within your campus context? Try to avoid being discouraged or derailed by potential costs at this point. You do not want to discount an idea before it is fully developed. There may be lower-cost options that can be worked out later. Or your campus advancement office may be able to fundraise to cover the costs. Even if something is not possible right away, having it documented as an idea can be important in the future. Once initial rollout of programming has success, you may be able to get additional resources to support further initiatives.

After identifying a strategy, prioritize implementation. What aspects can be enacted immediately with little or no financial cost? Who will be responsible for implementing and monitoring the first stage? When will next stages occur? How will administration be approached for needed resources? How will students, staff, and faculty be informed of new resources and policies?

CHAPTER 8

Sustaining Efforts Over Time

Trauma-Informed and Sensitive College (TISC) Model, Stage 4: Sustaining

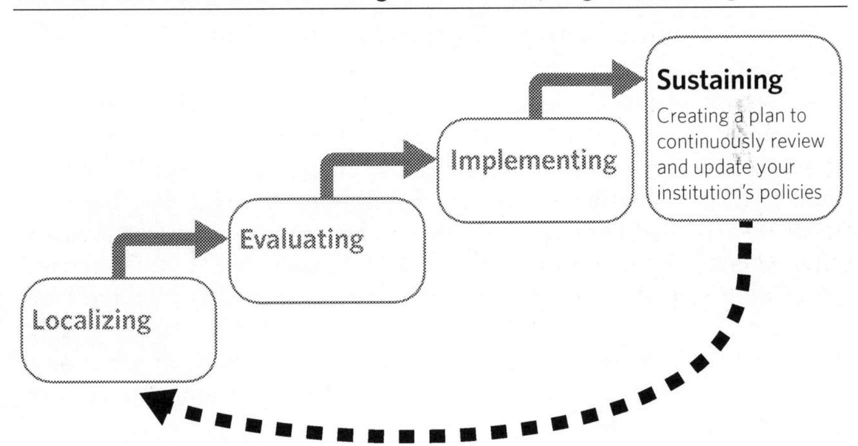

A trauma-informed approach involves shifting the institutional perspective. The entire institution focuses on how to support students experiencing basic needs insecurity and the multiple forms of trauma that may be associated with lacking housing security. Faculty, staff, and leadership all work collaboratively in maintaining a culture of support. Students will recognize a difference. As students begin to prosper, hopefully those employed by the institution will be encouraged that their efforts mattered. As we previously mentioned, all students benefit when institutions shift toward being trauma-informed because the educational spaces become more caring and supportive.

The first three stages of the trauma-informed model focus on gathering information and developing structures to support student retention and academic success. The sustaining stage involves continued review as well as supporting the services that were created. In this chapter, we provide guidance related to continuing the momentum generated during the first three stages.

AVOID ISOLATED SERVICES

The implementation stage involved developing support systems across campus in an integrated and comprehensive way. However, the support services can easily drift toward isolated endeavors without continued engagement with other services across campus. In particular, changes with services in one office on campus can have significant impacts on another. For example, if the SNAP support stops, then the food pantry may experience a higher volume of requests and the financial aid office may have more students requesting additional student aid to cover their expenses.

MAINTAIN COMMUNITY PARTNERSHIPS

We previously discussed the importance of working with community partners to identify and support student needs. These relationships need to be nurtured. Just as postsecondary institutions change over time, so do community agencies. Many rely on external funding that can be uncertain. Donations can increase or decrease. Staff and staff priorities change. Federal and state policies governing the services they provide may shift. Leadership and mission statements may evolve. Remaining in contact with these organizations increases the likelihood that higher education continues to be prioritized. In the event an organization needs to reduce or remove a support provided to students, it will be important for your institution to know before the change occurs.

Continuous collaboration with community agencies will also enable you to continue identifying student needs. Having agency representation on your committee can sustain linkages. If representation from community-based agencies shift, orient new partners as appropriate. Your institution should continuously be looking for new partnerships. Outreaching to new potential partners can bring renewed opportunities for students as well as provide new access points for service providers.

INTEGRATE BASIC NEEDS SECURITY INTO STRATEGIC PLANNING

Addressing student issues related to homelessness and housing insecurity should be integrated within the strategic planning process for your institution. One of the primary goals of strategic planning involves addressing student success and retention. Not only do student outcomes relate to the mission of the institution, but the current political context of higher education requires colleges and universities to demonstrate how they plan to retain students until graduation in order to justify the state, federal, and student financial investments in your institution. Reducing basic needs insecurity relates to increasing student retention.

CONNECT WITH ADVANCEMENT AND PHILANTHROPY OFFICES

While the evaluation process generally gets funded by the institution, there are opportunities to fundraise in order to sustain the programming. We encourage you to meet with the advancement or development office during this stage to identify a range of fundable opportunities related to basic needs insecurity. Many university donors, particularly alumni, have an interest in supporting programming and scholarships for students from underserved and low-income backgrounds. Some colleges and universities allow staff and faculty to have donations to programs like yours drawn directly from their payroll check. While potential donors may be unaware of homelessness and housing insecurity as issues on campus, advancement officers can present the idea to prospective donors who may be inclined to support such efforts. Since each campus will be slightly different, we present a few places to begin thinking about fundable opportunities. However, we encourage you to be creative in working with advancement to identify campus-specific areas to present to prospective donors.

As you consider involving donors, be cautious about how you leverage student voice in the process. Alumni love a good story. Be careful not to stigmatize students in promotional fundraising campaigns. Do use stories with the students' permission. Some students will openly tell their stories, but be careful to help them prepare for public attention and provide them options that involve keeping their identity confidential.

Food Vouchers and Pantry

In addition to partnering with a local food bank or community agency to stock the shelves, your campus may need additional support in the form of vouchers and staff. Vouchers can be particularly helpful as a supplement for students who are in the process of applying for social services supports as well as for those who do not qualify. Some students will need more support with food than can be provided by a food pantry. We have also found that food vouchers can be useful to provide for students during school breaks. A donor may be willing to provide financial support to cover these costs.

A larger donor may be willing provide an endowment to help fund the costs of a food pantry. These funds could be used to supplement the community food donations as well as fund a staff position. Many food pantries include staff who build relationships with the students while also connecting them with other supports on campus and in the community. A staff member can be particularly important in helping students apply for social services and food stamps. This level of donation could include a naming opportunity for the donor (e.g., The Rodriguez Food Support Center).

Students can also become developing philanthropists. Though programs should not be built on the backs of students, SWIPE programs, as mentioned in Chapter 7, can teach students that making investments in their communities in the form of donations is a meaningful role for them.

Emergency or Long-Term Housing

Some campuses have designated a few rooms in the residence halls as emergency housing for students. The length of time varies, but the general goal is to stabilize students while a plan is established. Although the housing units are on campus, costs still exist. The housing department on campus not only loses revenue from these spaces but there also may be costs associated with utilities. In addition, students seeking emergency housing may not have bedding or personal supplies. A donor may be interested in covering the costs associated with creating emergency housing for students on campus.

A larger donor may want to fund long-term housing for students experiencing housing insecurity. We are aware of one university that is working with a donor to create a housing unit for students exiting foster care, experiencing housing insecurity, and coming from low-income backgrounds. Obviously, such a venture would require a very large donation. However, a similar approach could involve covering the costs of on-campus housing or providing supplemental housing vouchers for students as part of the financial aid process.

Scholarships and Emergency Aid

Many donors are interested in scholarships that provide direct services to students as well as naming opportunities for the donor. We discourage having "homelessness" in the name of the scholarship. However, the eligibility requirements could be designed in a way to identify students who experienced housing insecurity in high school or have financially struggled in college. The financial aid office may be able to collaborate in creating parameters for the scholarship.

Financial aid officers also discuss the need for emergency aid for students after financial aid decisions have been made. In particular, there may be students who experience a crisis and need support that exceeds cost of attendance. Creating an emergency aid fund provides a resource for financial aid officers to draw from when a student has unmet needs that threaten their ability to be retained by the institution. Often, a relatively small amount of money can make the difference between the student remaining enrolled and stopping out of school.

In developing these efforts, work closely with financial aid to design scholarships that will not negatively impact the students' financial aid packages. Your financial aid administrators have expertise related to crafting scholarships and institutional grants that can be most beneficial to students.

Endowed Staff or Faculty Positions

Endowed staff and faculty positions allow the donor to shape the programming of the institution while also creating a naming opportunity. We previously discussed the importance of creating a single point of contact (SPOC) who coordinates services and works directly with students who experience basic needs insecurity. An endowed position allows for this position to become more permanently situated within the institutional structures. In particular, an endowed position would be protected during times of economic uncertainty for the institution or community. For example, many institutions cut supplemental services during the Great Recession beginning in 2008. However, it may be during such times that services related to basic needs insecurity may be most urgent for students.

An endowed faculty position may or may not include direct support for students. At a 4-year institution, this position could include conducting research related to basic needs insecurity and assisting the institution with continuous evaluation. The possibility exists that this position could include collaborating with the SPOC on campus to create and maintain supports. This faculty member could also serve as the liaison with other faculty members, including providing trainings and serving as an academic point of contact if a faculty member identifies a student in crisis.

PROVIDE TRAINING FOR FACULTY AND STAFF

Faculty come into direct contact with students every day. Students may share their personal challenges in class or during office hours, or an instructor may reach out to a student who has a significant change in behavior or a sudden drop in grades. While instructors often care about their students' personal and academic success, they are rarely equipped to support students. Given the significant challenges associated with housing insecurity, we would not expect instructors to be able to meet all of those needs. However, they should be informed of the services available. In particular, students may be more likely to seek the support if a trusted individual serves as a bridge. For campuses with a SPOC, the trainings may involve making sure all instructors know who this person is as well as what resources may be available.

Faculty may need to learn to assess for basic needs insecurity. Students who are falling asleep, grouchy, irritable, or not achieving may not be doing so because they partied too hard last night. They may not have eaten or have a place to stay. Faculty can ask about this when they engage students. Also, faculty can add notes in their syllabi about available services for basic needs.

Staff members may have different interactions with students, but often are in positions where students come to them in times of need. Each office has a particular area of focus and expertise. However, office staff should also be aware of the additional resources available and be encouraged to help students connect with other offices on campus as needed.

USE MEDIA TO ADVANCE YOUR MESSAGE

Partner with media outlets to draw attention to progress being made by the institution on the issues. Also, the media can be an important avenue to generate community partners and seek financial donations to support initiatives. Reframing the narrative about the "starving student" being a rite of passage to encourage more progressive thinking about the needs of students may require you to engage with media at many different levels. Create a concise, compelling message to prompt audiences to get involved at social, political, and financial levels. Develop short, clear talking points that ensure your message is consistent.

Look for reporters who have done recent stories on poverty, homelessness, and educational issues. Send them information about what you are doing. Consider print, radio, television, podcasts, and online media. If your institution has a media relations department, work with them. You can also connect with your student paper and radio programs.

Often, media outlets will want to highlight the voices of students. We encourage you to develop relationships with students who may be interested in these opportunities. Not all students will feel comfortable speaking about their challenges. However, there are often a few students on campus who become advocates. If you identify a SPOC on campus, you will want to help that individual become familiar with being interviewed by the media.

ADVOCATE FOR HIGHER EDUCATION POLICIES

Community partnerships are valuable throughout each of the stages we discussed in previous chapters. These individuals and agencies provide valuable information as well as services and support for your students. For example, your institution could not run a shelter for individuals experiencing homelessness or offer all of the services provided by Women,

Infant, and Children (WIC) programming. Just as these organizations support your students, they benefit from your advocacy as well. Be aware of proposed legislation that may indirectly influence the postsecondary aspirations of students (e.g., cuts in child care, food support, or emergency housing funding).

We also discussed the limited federal engagement related to homelessness and housing insecurity in higher education. At this point, the states have taken the lead in developing innovative policies for college students. Advocate for policies that have been successful in other states. If the political will does not exist at the state level, explore if the local community could implement similar policies. Work with legislators to develop policies that move away from emergency services and crisis intervention and toward prevention and higher education affordability.

Find out if the mayor in your local community has created initiatives related to homelessness and/or education. Try to get higher education representatives on those committees and be sure to attend the public meetings. Be sure local and state legislators hear your stories of success as well as the barriers limiting your ability to serve more students. When possible, invite students who want to share their stories with policymakers. You never want to force an individual to publicly discuss their traumas, and you never want to share their stories without explicitly gaining their permission. However, most campuses have students who emerge as advocates. Inviting them to share their story and design policy recommendations further empowers them.

Never underestimate the power of story. Your experiences as a professional and your students' personal stories have the potential to move forward policy issues in important ways. When needed, you can leverage media to get the attention of government officials as well as to mobilize the public who may not be aware of homelessness and housing insecurity on your campus.

MEET REGULARLY

The SPOC for your campus should not be expected to take complete ownership of designing and implementing supports. As we previous discussed, becoming a trauma-informed institution requires a comprehensive shift in how students experience your institution. In addition, you have professionals across campus who are experts in their given field. They will know about policy shifts and new programming ideas that could be implemented on your campus. They also have firsthand information about the challenges and successes of the program implementation strategy. While the SPOC may take a coordinating role, the committee you have developed as a part of this process should be maintained as an advisory team and should continue to meet on a regular basis. This standing committee could meet once a month at the beginning and then maybe move to once or twice a semester. You should continue including student voices and perspectives.

Consistent engagement with representatives across campus increases the likelihood that creative solutions and opportunities can be identified. In addition, gaps in support can more easily be identified when you have collaborative brainstorming conversations. Representatives across campus can provide informal reports about how things are going. As appropriate, the advisory team can provide informal or formal reports to the administration. You want to make sure to have advocates from across campus working on issues related to housing insecurity in order to ensure those efforts remain an institutional priority.

CONDUCT CONTINUOUS EVALUATION

We encourage you to consider evaluation a continuous process. The Great Recession beginning in 2008 demonstrated how quickly student needs, institutional resources, and community contexts can shift. In addition, local recruitment areas for an institution evolve over time. The student base you currently have may be significantly different in a decade.

State and federal policies also change over time. Federal and state financial aid requirements and funding can shift based upon the political priorities of those in office. To be honest, even maintaining the status quo can create challenges for students. The federal Pell Grant program has remained a consistent amount even as tuition and housing rates increase almost every year. If this continues into the future, the students' need relative to cost will increase even as they receive a consistent amount from the Pell Grant.

A committee should consistently meet to explore student needs as well as conducting periodic evaluations of the campus context. For example, a supplemental report could be written every 5 years with a more thorough data collection effort every 10 years.

CONCLUSION

Although creating new services can be exciting, sustaining effective programming is important. The goal should be to weave supports related to housing insecurity into the fabric of the institutional mission and daily operations. As administrative leadership shifts, you want these efforts to remain.

Application to Your Campus

- Develop a 5-to-10-year review plan. Having a formal plan in writing will be important.
- If you are planning to roll out services, what is the plan for doing that? How will the supports be developed in an integrated way?
- When would you recommend an interim report? When should a more thorough study be done? We recommend at least once every 10 years, which you may also want to align with strategic planning time frames in order to ensure this issue is part of that process. Or you could align with WASC or other accreditation reviews.

CHAPTER 9

Looking Forward

Addressing homelessness and housing insecurity among college students can seem overwhelming. We hope the previous chapters provided both encouragement and guidance as you continue developing supports intended to improve student retention. We provide a few final considerations to include on your journey of becoming a trauma-informed and sensitive college that meets the needs of students experiencing housing insecurity.

THIS WORK IS HARD, BUT IT MATTERS

We appreciate the amount of time, energy, and resources that needs to be dedicated to improve college access and retention for students experiencing homelessness and housing insecurity. Working collaboratively with colleagues across campus to shift organizational culture to be trauma-informed may require rethinking policies and practices that have been in place for decades. There may be individuals or groups at your institution who have vested interests in keeping current approaches in place. In addition, student outcomes may not be immediate. Housing insecurity and homelessness are complex social issues. Often, important shifts in practice take a few years to yield significant measurable impacts on student grades and retention.

While all of this may be true, it is also true that your work in this area matters. Please keep moving forward with these important initiatives. Remind administration of the importance of continuing to center housing insecurity and basic needs as institutional priorities. Continuing to meet with your colleagues across campus who are invested in this issue will also serve as an important source of encouragement.

And when you do get discouraged, reflect on the student voices in this book as well as those you have worked with over the years. They rely on your persistence, creativity, and commitment. These students directly benefit from the work that you do. Increasing their educational outcomes not only influences their future stability, but also has generational impacts as they raise children, connect with other family members who may face similar challenges, and excel and contribute in their communities. Your work matters.

TAKE CARE OF YOURSELF

Hearing the trauma of others can significantly impact you. Gathering the stories of individuals who have experienced homelessness, hunger, violence, abuse, or other personal crises has an impact on our cognitive functioning and personal well-being. Secondary trauma exists when we get negatively impacted by hearing and observing the trauma of other people. This is not about being a strong or weak person. Witnessing trauma influences everyone.

In addition to creating potential impacts related to stress, depression, and mental health, secondary trauma can lead to caregiver fatigue. At some point, most individuals working on topics like homelessness and housing insecurity will burn out if they are not intentional and disciplined about self-care. You are not alone in this. Building a community of professionals will be important. Find people who can share in your successes and setbacks as well as those who remind you to implement personal practices and boundaries that will enable you to continue this work for many years to come. Tyler Rodriguez works in the area of mindfulness and provides guidance concerning how to integrate self-care into the process of becoming a trauma-informed institution.

Self-Care Strategies for Educators

Tyler J. Rodriguez, *mindfulness, meditation, and yoga instructor*

The effects of secondary trauma can manifest in several different ways and in some cases may not show up immediately. Educators often put their personal needs aside for the immediate needs of students. In addition to building a community of support, you must make self-care a priority in order to maintain professional sustainability and prevent compassion fatigue.

Being able to separate yourself from the trauma experienced by your students is important. While empathy may motivate you to do this work, guilt or internalizing your students' trauma will lead to personal and professional burnout. Mindfulness and meditation practices are an accessible resource in self-care that can be used to prevent burnout and help reduce stress levels. Practicing mindfulness can be done at any time throughout the day and is a skill that is developed over time just like any other.

When the mind and body are present, secondary trauma has a more challenging time attaching itself because you are more aware of the present moment and allow yourself to take a step back from the current crisis. This separation should not be confused with disassociation from your students. In fact, you may be more able to address the issues at hand as you experience reduced mental and emotional fatigue, better decision making, and overall sustainability. Self-care looks different for everyone, but all self-care practice results in a deeper sense of gratitude and appreciation for oneself. As you develop a mindfulness practice, it is important to practice patience and care for yourself, just as you do with the people you are trying to help on a daily basis. Here are a few strategies I have found helpful:

Become Aware of Your Breath. This is the first and perhaps most common strategy. Becoming aware of the fact that you are actually breathing allows the mind to slow down and focus on one thing more intently as opposed to having the mind run wild from thought to thought with no clear direction in sight. Sit in a chair, take five deep cycles of breath, focus on the physical sensation of the breath moving in and out of your lungs and chest. With each cycle of breath, try to slow the breath down, relaxing more each time. Taking the time to focus on your breathing and nothing else will lay the building blocks for your mindfulness and self-care practice.

Complete a Body Scan. A second type of mindfulness practice that is readily available is completing a body scan. Sit in a chair or lie on your back with your eyes either closed or open and begin scanning your body for tension or stress from the top of the head down to the feet. Start by focusing on major body parts such as top of head, forehead, cheek bones, throat, chest, all the way down to feet. Depending on the time available, the body scan can be completed in great detail or simplicity. The same common denominator exists in this type of mindfulness practice in that you are consciously directing the mind's attention to specific points.

Notice Your Surroundings. The body scan can also be done while taking a walk, at your desk, washing the dishes, or simply relaxing at home. In this regard, take notice of your immediate environment. What does the environment around you look like? What is the temperature of the air, how does it feel on your skin? What colors and sounds do you notice? You'll soon notice that when you take time to notice your environment and take in the sensations with purposeful attention, your mind and body become more calm and centered, even if just for a moment.

Take Time for Yourself. Write down 10 things that you enjoy doing throughout your day that make you feel good—for example, making a cup of tea, going for a walk, journaling, sitting outside for a few minutes, calling a friend or relative, and so on. Carve out time in your day to do at least one of those things without any distractions and then observe how you feel or write it down in a journal. Take time to fill your cup before your cup is empty. You and your relationships will benefit from this simple and overlooked yet powerful reminder.

SHARE YOUR STORY

As you develop and implement approaches to improve educational outcomes for students experiencing housing insecurity on your campus, you will gather important insights and learn valuable lessons. We encourage you to keep track of both the successes and setbacks that occur along the way. You will identify creative solutions that differ from what we have discussed.

Be sure to share your story with other postsecondary institutions and community agencies across the country. Consider writing up a monograph or digital pamphlet that can be distributed easily to colleges and universities across the country. You could also blog about the process or utilize social media to distribute lessons learned. In addition, share information on your institutional website with contact information for people working closely with the programs and services.

We also hope that you mentor other institutions as they become aware of housing insecurity on their campuses and need guidance. Just as we encouraged you to reach out to institutions when you were early in the process, you will also have an opportunity to serve in that role. Together, we are a community—a movement for change and support for our students.

APPENDIX A

Measuring Homelessness and Housing Insecurity

In the past 30 days (12 months), have you slept in any of the following places? Please check all that apply.

- ☐ Campus or university housing
- ☐ Sorority/fraternity house
- ☐ In a rented or owned house, mobile home, or apartment (alone or with roommates or friends)
- ☐ In a rented or owned house, mobile home, or apartment with my family (parent, guardian, or relative)
- ☐ At a shelter
- ☐ In a camper
- ☐ Temporarily staying with a relative, friend, or couch surfing until I find other housing
- ☐ Temporarily at a hotel or motel without a permanent home to return to (not on vacation or business travel)
- ☐ In transitional housing or independent living program
- ☐ At a group home such as halfway house or residential program for mental health or substance abuse
- ☐ At a treatment center (such as detox, hospital, and so on)
- ☐ Outdoor location such as street, sidewalk, or alley; bus or train stop; campground or woods; park, beach, or riverbed; under bridge or overpass
- ☐ In a closed area/space with a roof not meant for human habitation such as abandoned building, car or truck, van, RV, or camper, encampment or tent, or unconverted garage, attic, or basement

In the past 30 days (12 months), how many nights did you sleep in any of the following places because you did not have a fixed, regular, and adequate nighttime residence? Choose between 0 and 30 nights.

- ☐ At a shelter
- ☐ In a camper
- ☐ In transitional housing or independent living program
- ☐ At a group home such as halfway house or residential program for mental health or substance abuse
- ☐ At a treatment center (such as detox, hospital, and so on)
- ☐ Outdoor location such as street, sidewalk, or alley; bus or train stop; campground or woods; park, beach, or riverbed; under bridge or overpass
- ☐ In a closed area/space with a roof not meant for human habitation such as abandoned building; car or truck, van, RV, or camper; encampment or tent; or unconverted garage, attic, or basement
- ☐ Temporarily staying with a relative, friend, or couch surfing until I find other housing
- ☐ Temporarily at a hotel or motel without a permanent home to return to (not on vacation or business travel)

Assessing Student Supports

To learn more about supports and resources that students access on and off campus, ask students about usage patterns. We provide some campus-based resources we know matter, but encourage you to refine this list based upon your campus context.

Do you use any of the following campus-based resources? Mark all that apply.	Never heard of it/not offered at my campus	Heard of it, but never used it	Used it in the past	Currently use it
Food pantry (somewhere on campus to get free food)				
Campus community gardens				
CalFresh application assistance ("food stamps"/EBT)				
EBT at a market on campus				
Campus emergency housing services				
Student psychological counseling center				
Student health center				

If you do not use any of these resources, please indicate why. Mark all that apply.

- ☐ I am not eligible for the programs
- ☐ I have not heard of the programs
- ☐ I do not need assistance
- ☐ I do not have time to access these resources

- ☐ I do not know how to access these resources
- ☐ I do not believe in using social services
- ☐ It is embarrassing to have to use these resources
- ☐ I do not have transportation
- ☐ Other

Do you use any of the following public benefits or off-campus community resources? Mark all that apply.	Never heard of it/ not offered at my campus	Heard of it, but never used it	Used it in the past	Currently use it
CalFresh ("food stamps"/EBT)				
Off-campus food pantry/food bank				
Off-campus community garden				
Emergency meal program				
Homeless shelter				
Transitional living				
Subsidized housing, (i.e., HUD/ Housing Choice Voucher formerly known as Section 8)				
CalWorks				
WIC				
TANF				
SSI				
SSDI				
Medicaid				
Child-care assistance				
Unemployment insurance				
Utility assistance				
Earned Income Tax Credit (EITC)				
Veteran's benefits				

If you do not use any of these resources, please indicate why. Mark all that apply.

- ☐ I am not eligible for the programs
- ☐ I have not heard of the programs
- ☐ I do not need assistance
- ☐ I do not have time to access these resources
- ☐ I do not know how to access these resources
- ☐ I do not believe in using social services
- ☐ It is embarrassing to have to use social services
- ☐ I do not have transportation
- ☐ Other

Meeting Students' Basic Needs

Background questions

- Please tell me a little about your life right now.
- Please describe your college experience.

Food and housing

- Where have you been living during your college/university experience? How long did you live there? How often did you move?
- Please describe your access to food.

Support

- What has helped you succeed in college?
- What other resources or opportunities assisted you in staying in college?
- What relationships or connections to people did you have that assisted you in staying in college?

Barriers

- What are things that have kept you from succeeding in college? What obstacles have you faced?

Ideas or suggestions on how to improve the college experience

- What could others do to help you or other students living with similar circumstances to best handle college?
- Is there anything else that you want to tell me about your experiences of being in college?

California State University, Long Beach, Basic Needs Program

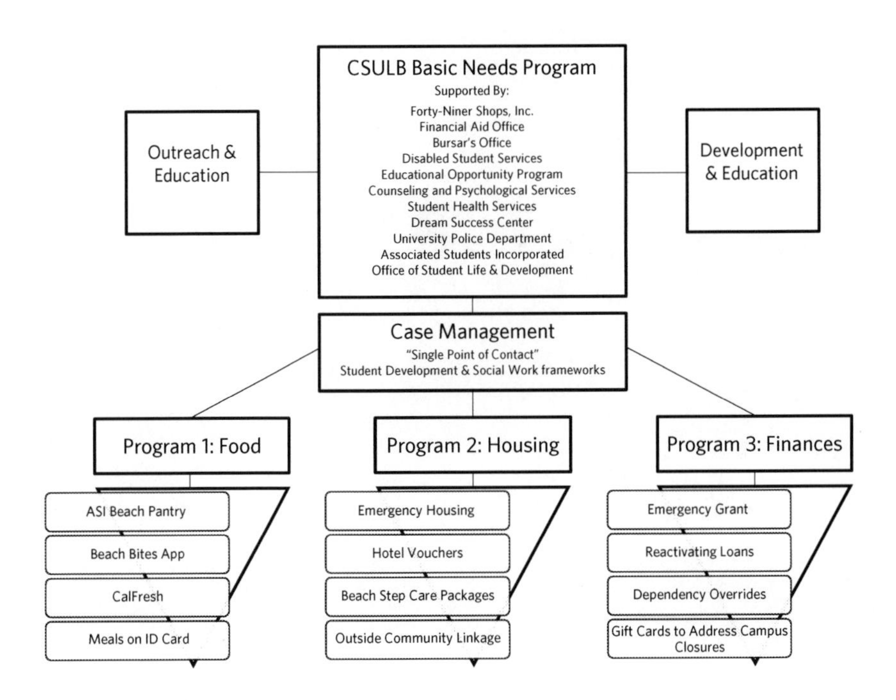

References

Ambrose, V. K. (2016). *"It's like a mountain": The lived experiences of homeless college students* (Doctoral dissertation). University of Tennessee.

Au, N., & Hyatt, S. (2017). *Resources supporting homeless students at California's public universities and college.* California Homeless Youth Project. Retrieved from cahomelessyouth.library.ca.gov/docs/pdf/collegesupportsreportpdf4-27-17.pdf

Babcock, E., & Ruize de Luzuriaga, N. (2016). *Families disrupting the cycle of poverty: Coaching with an intergenerational lens.* Boston, MA: Economic Mobility Pathways.

Barker, J. (2016). A habitus of instability: Youth homelessness and instability. *Journal of Youth Studies, 19*(5), 665–683.

Bradburn, N., Sudman, S., & Wansink, B. (2004). *Asking questions: The definitive guide to questionnaire design* (Rev. ed.). San Francisco, CA: Jossey-Bass.

Broton, K. M., & Goldrick-Rab, S. (2018). Going without: An exploration of food and housing insecurity among undergraduates. *Educational Researcher, 47*(2),121–133.

Cady, C. L. (2014). Food insecurity as a student issue. *Journal of College and Character, 14*(4), 265–271.

California Homeless Youth Project. (2018). *Supporting California's homeless & low-income college students: A practical.* Author. Retrieved from www2.calstate.edu/impact-of-the-csu/student-success/basic-needs-initiative/Documents/5GuidesToHelpHomelessCollegeStudents.pdf

Center for Youth Wellness. (2014). *An unhealthy dose of stress: The impact of adverse childhood experiences and toxic stress on childhood health and development.* San Francisco, CA: Author.

Coates, J., & McKenzie-Mohr, S. (2010). Out of the frying pan, into the fire: Trauma in the lives of homeless youth prior to and during homelessness. *Journal of Sociology & Social Welfare, 37*(4), 65–96.

Cole, S. F., O'Brien, J. G., Gadd, M. G., Ristuccia, J., Wallace, D. L., & Gregory, M. (2005). *Helping traumatized children learn: Supportive school environments for children traumatized by family violence.* Boston, MA: Massachusetts Advocates for Children.

Craig, S. E. (2016). *Trauma-sensitive schools: Learning communities transforming children's lives, K–5.* New York, NY: Teachers College Press.

Craig, S. E. (2017). *Trauma-sensitive schools for the adolescent years: Promoting resiliency and healing, grades 6–12.* New York, NY: Teachers College Press.

Crutchfield, R. (2016). *Serving displaced and food insecure students in the CSU.* California State University Office of the Chancellor. Retrieved from www.calstate.edu/AcadAff/documents/ServingDisplacedandFoodInsecureStudetnsintheCSUJanuary20163.8.16.pdf

Crutchfield, R. M., Chambers, R. M., & Duffield, B. (2016). Jumping through the hoops to get financial aid for college students who are homeless: Policy analysis of the College Cost Reduction and Access Act of 2007. *Families in Society: The Journal of Contemporary Social Services, 97*(3), 191–199.

Crutchfield, R. M., & Maguire, J. (2017). Researching basic needs in higher education: Qualitative and quantitative instruments to explore a holistic understanding of food and housing insecurity. California State University Office of the Chancellor. Retrieved from www2.calstate.edu/impact-of-the-csu/student-success/basic needs-initiative/Documents/researching-basic-needs.pdf

Crutchfield, R. M., & Maguire, J. (2018). *California State University Office of the Chancellor study of student basic needs.* Retrieved from www.calstate.edu/basicneeds

Crutchfield, R. M., & Maguire, J. (2019). *California State University Office of the Chancellor study of student service access and basic needs.* Retrieved from www.calstate.edu/basicneeds

Dill, V. S., & Lee, C. (2016). Homeless and college-bound. *Educational Leadership, 73*(6), 42–47.

Dukes, C. (2013). *College access and success for students experiencing homelessness: A toolkit for educators and service providers.* Greensboro, NC: National Center for Homeless Education.

Erdur-Baker, O., Aberson, C. L., Barrow, J. C., & Draper, M. R. (2006). Nature and severity of college students' psychological concerns: A comparison of clinical and nonclinical national samples. *Professional Psychology: Research and Practice, 37*, 317–323.

Goldrick-Rab, S. (2016). *Paying the price: College costs, financial aid, and the betrayal of the American dream.* Chicago, IL: University of Chicago Press.

Goldrick-Rab, S., Broton, K., & Eisenberg, D. (2015). *Hungry to learn: Addressing food and housing insecurity among undergraduates.* Madison: University of Wisconsin, Wisconsin HOPE Lab.

Goldrick-Rab, S., Cady, C., & Coca, V. (2018). *Campus food pantries: Insights from a national survey.* Philadelphia, PA: The Temple University Hope Center.

Goldrick-Rab, S., Richardson, J., & Hernandez, A. (2017). *Hungry and homeless in college: Results from a national study of basic needs insecurity in higher education.* Madison: University of Wisconsin, Wisconsin HOPE Lab.

Goldrick-Rab, S., Richardson, J., & Kinsley, P. (2017). *Guide to assessing basic needs insecurity in higher education.* Madison: University of Wisconsin, Wisconsin HOPE Lab.

Gupton, J. T. (2017). Campus of opportunity: A qualitative analysis of homeless students in community college. *Community College Review, 45*(3), 190–214.

Hallett, R. E. (2012). *Educational experiences of hidden homeless teenagers: Living doubled-up.* New York, NY: Routledge.

Hallett, R. E., & Crutchfield, R. M. (2017). *Homelessness and housing insecurity in higher education: A trauma-informed approach to research, policy, and practice (ASHE Higher Education Report, (43)*6). Boston, MA: Jossey-Bass.

Hallett, R. E., & Freas, A. (2018). Community college students' experiences with homelessness and housing insecurity. *Community College Journal of Research and Practice, 42*(10), 724–739.

Hallett, R. E., Freas, A., & Mo, E. (2018). The case for a single point of contact for college students experiencing homelessness. *New Directions for Community Colleges, 2018*(184), 39–49.

Hallett, R. E., & Skrla, L. (2017). *Serving students who are homeless: A resource guide for schools, districts, and educational leaders.* New York, NY: Teachers College Press.

Hope Center for College, Community and Justice. (2018). *Real college: A study of the real experiences of college students.* Retrieved on December 28, 2018 from drive.google.com/file/d/1RplSIrNUO9Oy0BzVSsstjAm4zkZDeDhz/view

Hopper, E. K., Bassuk, E. L., & Olivet, J. (2010). Shelter from the storm: Trauma-informed care in homeless service settings. *Open Health Services and Policy Journal, 3*, 80–100.

Hyatt, S., Walzer, B., & Julianelle, P. (2014). *California's homeless students: A growing population.* Sacramento, CA: California Homeless Project.

Johnson, S. B., Riley, A. W., Granger, D. A., & Riis, J. (2013). The science of early life toxic stress for pediatric practice and advocacy. *Pediatrics, 131*, 319–327.

Krosnick, J. A., & Presser, S. (2010). Questions and questionnaire design. In P. V. Marsden & J. D. Wright (Eds.), *Handbook of Survey Research* (2nd ed., pp. 263–313). Biggleswade, United Kingdom: Emerald Group.

Massachusetts Department of Higher Education. (2017). *2016 survey of Massachusetts public colleges and universities: Student hunger and homelessness.* Boston, MA: Author.

Miller, P. M. (2011a). A critical analysis of the research on student homelessness. *Review of Educational Research, 81*(3), 308–337.

Miller, P. M. (2011b). An examination of the McKinney–Vento Act and its influence on the homeless education situation. *Education Policy, 25*(3), 424–450.

National Association for the Education of Homeless Children and Youth (NAEHCY). (2018). *Single point-of-contact model.* Retrieved from naehcy.org/wp-content/uploads/2018/08/SPOC-Model-Revamp-FINAL.pdf

National Center for Homeless Education (NCHE). (2017). *Homelessness reported for federal student aid applicants.* Greensboro: University of North Carolina–Greensboro. Retrieved from nche.ed.gov/downloads/he/fafsa-homeless-2016-2017.pdf

National Child Traumatic Stress Network. (2014). *Complex trauma: Facts for educators.* Retrieved from www.nctsn.org/sites/default/files/assets/pdfs/complext_trauma_facts_educators_final.pdf

Nazmi, A., Martinez, S., Byrd, A., Robinson, D., Bianco, S., Maguire, J., . . . Ritchie, L. (2018, June 22). A systematic review of food insecurity among US students in higher education. *Journal of Hunger & Environmental Nutrition.* doi:10.1080/19320248.2018.1484316

Newfield, C. (2018). *The great mistake: How we wrecked public universities and how we can fix them.* Baltimore, MD: John Hopkins University Press.

Pavlakis, A. E. (2014). Living and learning at the intersection: Student homelessness and complex policy environments. *The Urban Review, 46*(3), 445–475.

Perkins, M., & Graham-Bermann, S. (2012). Violence exposure and the development of school-related functioning: Mental health, neurocognition, and learning. *Aggression and Violent Behavior, 17*(1), 89–98.

Schaeffer, N. C., & Presser, S. (2003). The science of asking questions. *Annual Review of Sociology*, *29*, 65–88.

Schmitz, R. M. (2016). *On the street and on campus: A comparison of life course trajectories among homeless and college lesbian, gay, bisexual, transgender and queer young adults* (Unpublished doctoral dissertation). University of Nebraska–Lincoln.

Silva, M. R., Kleinert, W. L., Sheppard, A. V., Cantrell, K. A., Freeman-Coppadge, D. J., Tsoy, E., . . . Pearrow, M. (2017). The relationship between food security, housing stability, and school performance among college students in an urban university. *Journal of College Student Retention*, *19*(3), 284–299.

Steele, W., & Malchiodi, C. A. (2012). *Trauma-informed practices with children and adolescents*. New York, NY: Routledge.

Tierney, W. G., Gupton, J. T., & Hallett, R. E. (2008). *Transition to adulthood for homeless adolescents*. Los Angeles, CA: Center for Higher Education Policy Analysis.

Tierney, W. G., & Hallett, R. E. (2012). Social capital and homeless youth: Influence of residential instability on college access. *Metropolitan Universities Journal*, *22*(3), 46–62.

Tsui, E., Freudenberg, N., Manzo, L., Jones, H., Kwan, A., & Gagnon, M. (2011). *Housing instability at CUNY: Results from a survey of CUNY undergraduate students*. New York, NY: City University of New York.

Twill, S. E., Bergdahl, J., & Fensler, R. (2016). Partnering to build a pantry: A university campus responds to student food insecurity. *Journal of Poverty*, *20*(3), 340–358

University of California Global Food Initiative. (2017). *Global food initiative: Food and housing security at the University of California*. Retrieved from ucop.edu/global-food-initiative/_files/food-housing-security.pdf

U.S. Department of Health and Human Services. (2000, November). *Measuring healthy days: Population assessment of health-related quality of life*. Retrieved from www.cdc.gov/hrqol/pdfs/mhd.pdf

U. S. Department of Housing and Urban Development (HUD). (2015). *Barriers to success: Housing insecurity for US college students*. Washington, DC: Author. Retrieved from www.huduser.gov/portal/periodicals/insight/insight_2.pdf

Wolch, J., Dear, M., Blasi, G., Flaming, D., Tepper, P., Koegel, P. (with Warshawsky, D.). (2007, January 30). *Ending homelessness in Los Angeles: Inter-university consortium against homelessness*. Los Angeles: University of Southern California, USC Center for Safer Cities.

Wood, J. L., Harris, F., III, & Delgado, N. R. (2017). *Struggling to survive—striving to succeed: Food and housing insecurities in the community college*. San Diego, CA: Community College Equity Assessment Lab.

Index

The letter *f* or t following a page number refers to a figure or table, respectively.

About the Authors

Ronald Hallett is a professor of organizational leadership in the LaFetra College of Education at the University of La Verne and a research associate in the Pullias Center for Higher Education at the University of Southern California. A former school teacher, he now researches the educational experiences that marginalized youth face in their pursuit of completing high school and transitioning to college. Specifically, he has spent over a decade studying the educational experiences of youth experiencing homelessness. In addition to publishing several research articles and book chapters on the topic, he recently authored or coauthored three books related to youth homelessness: *Educational Experiences of Hidden Homeless Teenagers* (Routledge, 2012); *Serving Students Who Are Homeless: A Resource Guide for Schools, Districts, and Educational Leaders* (with Linda Skrla, Teachers College Press, 2016); and *Homelessness and Housing Insecurity in Higher Education* (with Rashida Crutchfield, ASHE Higher Education Report Series, 2018).

Rashida Crutchfield is an associate professor in the School of Social Work at California State University, Long Beach. She previously served on the staff of Covenant House California, a shelter for homeless 18-to-24-year-olds. This experience gave her insight into practice and building rapport and intervention with this population's strengths, needs, and perspectives. Her areas of practice and research focus on youth homelessness, access to higher education, social and economic development, and social work community practice. She has authored or coauthored several research articles, including "Jumping Through the Hoops to Get Financial Aid for College Students Who Are Homeless: Policy Analysis of The College Cost Reduction and Access Act of 2007" in *Families in Society* and "Under a Temporary Roof and in the Classroom: Service Agencies For Youth Who Are Homeless While Enrolled in Community College" in *Child & Youth Services*. She was the principal investigator for Phase 1 and is a co-principal investigator for Phases 2 and 3 of the California State University Study of Student Basic Needs.

Jennifer Maguire is an associate professor in the Department of Social Work at Humboldt State University. She is an advocate and scholar who works to contribute to creating a public higher education system where all college and university students have their basic needs met while earning a degree. Prior to entering academia, she was a wraparound social worker with Humboldt County, California, Department of Health and Human Services, Child Welfare Services (CWS), and worked closely with foster youth transitioning to independent living situations. She observed the youth she worked with experience systemic barriers to finding stable housing so significant that even imagining earning a college degree often seemed impossible. Her work supporting foster and former foster youth to navigate the public education and social services systems helped inspire her future work. She is co-principal investigator for Phases 2 and 3 of the California State University Study of Student Basic Needs.